KU-693-210

# C o n t e n t s

## KEY TO MAPS

✈       Airport
D50     Road number
★       Start of walk/tour
〰〰     Ancient walls
ⓘ       Information
☀       Viewpoint
240m▲   Mountain
✝       Church

# Introduction

From the 11th to the 13th centuries, Normandy, the coastal region lying to the northwest of Paris, was a powerful state in northern France. Peopled by hard-working, stubborn and conservative Scandinavians, it produced William, Duke of Normandy, and came to represent law and order, great castles and church builders. Despite being absorbed into France in 1449, then losing its status as a separate province after the French Revolution, Normandy is still recognised as a special area.

Colourful boats line the Cherbourg marina

Normandy is now split into five *départements*: Manche, Calvados, Orne, Eure and Seine-Maritime. After the ravages of World War II, nearly 600 towns had to be rebuilt; today, despite unemployment, there is still an overall look of affluence to the market towns and cities.

For some, the straight-from-the-sea fish and shellfish are reason enough to visit; for others it's the beef and *pré-salé*

## Normandy

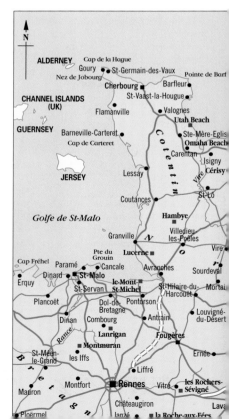

# NORMANDY

BY

KATHY ARNOLD & PAUL WADE

Produced by
Thomas Cook Publishing

**Written by** Kathy Arnold & Paul Wade
**Updated by** Juliette Rogers
**Original photography by** Rob Moore
**Original design by** Laburnum Technologies Pvt Ltd

**Editing and page layout by** Cambridge Publishing
Management Ltd, Unit 2, Burr Elm Court,
Caldecote CB3 7NU
**Series Editor:** Karen Beaulah

Published by Thomas Cook Publishing
A division of Thomas Cook Tour Operations Ltd
Company Registration No. 1450464 England

PO Box 227, The Thomas Cook Business Park,
Unit 18, Coningsby Road,
Peterborough PE3 8SB, United Kingdom
E-mail: books@thomascook.com
www.thomascookpublishing.com
Tel: +44 (0)1733 416477

ISBN-13: 978-1-84157-702-9
ISBN-10: 1-84157-702-2

First edition © 2003 Thomas Cook Publishing
Reprinted 2004
Second edition © 2006 Thomas Cook Publishing

Project Editor: Diane Ashmore
Production/DTP Editor: Steven Collins

Printed and bound in Spain by: Grafo Industrias Gráficas, Basauri.

Cover design by: Liz Lyons Design, Oxford.
Front cover credits: Left © Bethune Carmichael/Lonely Planet; centre © Getty;
right © Jon Arnold Images/PhotoLibrary
Back cover credits: Left © Robert Harding Picture Library Ltd/PhotoLibrary;
right © Robert Haines/Alamy

lamb, the rich cream sauces and renowned cheeses. Some come on pilgrimages: to Lisieux, and its basilica of the modern Saint Theresa; to Giverny, the home and gardens of the Impressionist painter Claude Monet; or to the D-Day beaches where family and friends fell in the Battle of Normandy in 1944.

French families come for their summer holidays as they have for nearly two centuries, ever since sea-bathing became fashionable. Thousands head inland, where small farms in peaceful, wooded valleys are a strong reminder of their roots. Then there are the cultural tourists, whisked by bus from the glory of Mont-St-Michel to the Bayeux Tapestry and on to Rouen's epic cathedral.

To savour the real Normandy you must drive the backroads, cycle on lanes through the *bocage* (hedged fields), shop in a market, stroll along cobbled streets, and admire a small church. Only then can you truly discover the character and fascinating history of this distinctive part of France.

## Normandy region

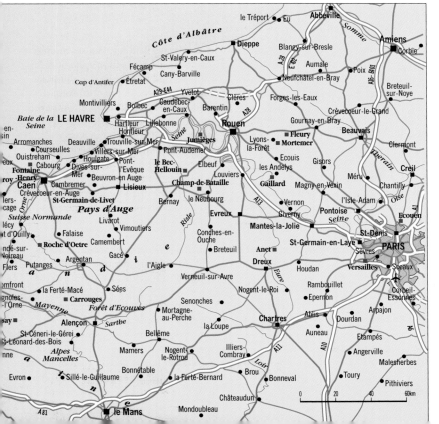

# The land

From Mont-St-Michel on the Brittany border to Rouen is 245km (152 miles); more specifically, some three million Normans live in an area about the same size as Belgium, whose population is three times greater. Normandy is administratively divided into the Regions of Haute (Upper) and Basse (Lower) Normandy. Roughly speaking, 'Haute' refers to the area bordering the River Seine, centred on Rouen; the rest is 'Basse'. Coastal Normandy contrasts with inland, while the whole is sliced by rivers ranging from the internationally known Seine to smaller waterways like the Eure and Orne, the Dives and Touques. In this book Normandy is divided into four areas.

A sublime sunset on the chalk cliffs at Étretat, north of Le Havre

### Northeastern Normandy

This includes Le Havre and Rouen and is bordered by the River Seine. The Caux (chalk) region has expansive sugar-beet fields and white coastal cliffs. Inland are the vast beech forests of Eawy and Lyons, as well as the fertile meadows of the Seine valley, which produce fruits and berries.

### Central Normandy

Think of half-timbered cottages, cows and apple orchards; you will find them in the Pays d'Auge, where every bend in the road produces another idyllic-looking scene. Around Caen, the land is open and flat. To the south, limestone is quarried, then the land drops away to the hills of the Suisse Normande (Norman Switzerland), with its small, almost hidden, wooded river valleys.

### Western Normandy

The Cotentin Peninsula is an out-thrust of the Armorican Massif that also characterises Brittany. Houses huddle together, sheltering from Atlantic gales, yet Granville and Carteret are popular summer resorts. In the northwest corner, coastal bluffs drop down to the sea, but inland and southwards the landscape softens into the *bocage*, a patchwork quilt of small fields seamed by dense hedges. Mont-St-Michel is a familiar sight, a natural outcrop of granite, while the southeast corner around Carentan is marshland, criss-crossed with dikes.

### Southern Normandy and Le Mans

This extends past the traditional boundary to include Le Mans and the Alpes Mancelles (the Le Mans Alps), not snowcapped peaks but a forested roller-coaster of hills and dales.

### The coasts

Normandy boasts 600km (373 miles) of coastline, including some evocatively named stretches: the Côte d'Albâtre (Alabaster Coast) between Étretat and Dieppe; the Côte Fleurie (Flower Coast) from the River Seine to the Orne River, with Trouville and Deauville; and the Côte de Nacre (Mother-of-Pearl Coast), where sand and sea shimmer in shades ranging from silver-blue to grey-green.

## Vantage points

Two hills claim to be the highest point in western France, both near Alençon. To the west is the Mont des Avaloirs in Mayenne; northwest is the signal station in the Écouves Forest: both are 417m (1,368 ft) high. Tiny lanes criss-cross the countryside, often without signposts at intersections. Guess which turning to take, and remember that getting lost is half the fun.

## Climate

With the Atlantic Ocean to the west, the prevailing winds are the moist, mild southwesterlies. The intense green pastures result from cool, wet winters and mild summers with a regular sprinkling of rain.

## Flora and fauna

There is more to Normandy than just cattle and horses. Some forests harbour roe and red deer; you will hear tits, thrushes and warblers, joined by nightingales and woodpeckers.

In spring, purple orchids and yellow primroses colour hedges, while the fields glint with cowslips. On the Cotentin Peninsula, sea thrift and spurge provide a pink and green patchwork, sea holly grows spiky and dusty purple, while marram holds the sand dunes together. In autumn, shearwaters, gulls and gannets soar overhead on their way south; in the marshes round Carentan, waders and wildfowl alight to shelter in the reeds.

The Suisse Normande looks and feels a lot different from 'typical' Normandy

## Seafarers

A thousand years ago, the adventure-loving Vikings of Scandinavia sought new territory for their growing population. In their *drakkars* (longboats) they pillaged every estuary around the North Sea and beyond. After the death of Charlemagne, King of the Franks, Normandy presented a soft target and, in 841, these Norsemen, Northmen, or Normans as they came to be called, sailed up the River Seine to pillage Rouen. By 911, their attacks were so frequent that King Charles the Simple of France gave in to Hrølf (Rollo). With the Treaty of St-Clair-sur-Epte, Normandy was exchanged for Viking allegiance, conversion to Christianity and a promise to halt further attacks. Some of these invaders stayed, and names like Dieppe, Caudebec and Langrune (deep, cold-stream and green-land) are a legacy. In later centuries, the Normans were to colonise parts of the Mediterranean, Africa and the New World.

## Minority rule

The swift transformation from colony to kingdom between 911 and 1066 is quite remarkable. In a mere 150 years, rampaging invaders turned into highly organised Frenchmen. Rollo and his companions were Norwegians who moved in as the ruling class. Soon, Danes took advantage of their fellow Scandinavians' good fortune to move into the towns but the bulk of the population were still Franks. It was the invaders who gave up their pagan beliefs to embrace Frankish Christianity, the invaders who enforced local laws and the invaders who slowly abandoned their native tongue in favour of French. By the time that Duke William (himself a bastard) fought at

HIC SEPULTUS EST
INVICTISSIMUS
GUILLELMUS
CONQUESTOR.
NORMANNIÆ DUX,
ET ANGLIÆ REX,
HUJUS CE DOMUS.
CONDITOR.
QUI OBIIT ANNO
M.LXXXVII.

the Battle of Hastings, his people were called the Franci or French as Panel 53 of the Bayeux Tapestry records.

## The most famous Norman of all

The Normans were a dynamic people, full of ideas and strong on organisation. Even today, they are regarded as the 'lawyers of France' for their love of rules and regulations. The high point of Norman civilisation came in the 11th century under William the Conqueror (*see p63*), an excellent soldier, a clever legislator and a charismatic leader.

## A land of war

After William became King of England in 1066, Normandy was ruled by English kings off and on until the end of the Hundred Years' War in 1450. Then there were religious struggles, since the Normans, like their Protestant fellow northern Europeans, were in conflict with the Roman Catholics. Many Normans supported the monarchy after the French Revolution of 1789, leading to yet more strife. Following the Revolution, the province of Normandy disappeared, to be replaced by five *départements*. The name of Normandy came back into government recognition in the 1980s with the introduction of regional-level administrations, and today Upper and Lower are working on ways to pool their resources and bureaucracies, to make Normandy one again. Duke William would have been proud.

## Normans today

The outsider would find it impossible to distinguish 'Normans' from other French people: they dress, eat and drive much the same, even if they consume more cream and butter than the rest of the country. They tend to be a little reserved, but a smile and a handshake is usually enough to break the ice. 'In the south of France, they are more open, make lots of promises . . . which they never keep,' as one Norman summed it up, 'whereas we take our time about whether we'll do something. But we'll never break a promise.'

Facing page above: doorway with faces in Brucheville; below: the Conqueror's tomb, Church of St-Etienne, Caen
Below: fisherman at St-Vaast-la Houge

# History

| | |
|---|---|
| **900 BC** | The Celts move into what is now Normandy. |
| **56 BC** | Roman Conquest: Savinius defeats local chieftain Viridorix. As Roman rule strengthens, towns like *Mediolanum* (Évreux) and *Noviomagus* (Lisieux) develop, with *Rotomagus* (Rouen) as the capital of the region. |
| **2nd to 3rd centuries** | Christianity arrives, thanks to saints like Martin and Germanus among others. Many Norman villages still bear their names. |
| **486** | As the Roman Empire collapses, the Franks move in. King Clovis takes over Rouen and Évreux. Later, his son Clothaire rules the Western Kingdom of Neustria. |
| **6th to 8th centuries** | Monasteries are built in the Seine valley; the network of monastic communities grows in size, influence and wealth. St-Wandrille Abbey is founded in 649, Mont-St-Michel in 708. |
| **841** | Rouen is burned to the ground by the Vikings whose raids have become bolder, attacking first the coastal settlements, then sailing up the River Seine to Rouen and beyond. |
| **911** | Normandy, as we know it, is created by the Treaty (no more than a handshake) at St-Clair-sur-Epte. Rollo, Hrølf the Walker, becomes the first Duke of Normandy. Soon after, serfdom is abolished. |
| **1027** | The birth of an illegitimate son, William, to Robert the Magnificent, Duke of Normandy. Aged seven, the boy succeeds his father; William the Bastard becomes duke and, later, William the Conqueror. |
| **1066** | William invades England, defeats King Harold at the Battle of Hastings and is crowned King of England. |
| **1087** | William dies in Rouen and is buried in the Abbaye aux Hommes he founded in Caen. |

| | |
|---|---|
| **12th to 15th centuries** | The kings of France and England fight over Normandy. Since the Conquest, English monarchs own the Duchy of Normandy; their marriages bring them more French territory and even a claim to the French throne. |
| **1152** | After marrying Eleanor of Aquitaine, King Henry II of England rules one-third of France. |
| **1259** | In the Treaty of Paris, King Henry III renounces his claim to Normandy. |
| **1337** | Start of the Hundred Years' War with England. |
| **1431** | Joan of Arc is burned at the stake in Rouen. |
| **1450** | End of the Hundred Years' War. Thanks to King Charles VII's victory at Formigny on 15 April, Normandy is finally ceded to France. |
| **1517** | To strengthen France's international communications, King François I commissions the new port of Le Havre at the mouth of the River Seine. |

**1589** Protestant King Henry IV of France defeats the Catholics at Ivry-la-Bataille, near Évreux. The Wars of Religion are ended by the Edict of Nantes, 1598, which grants limited but significant rights to Huguenots (Protestants).

Normandy's hero: William the Conqueror on the attack in Falaise

| | |
|---|---|
| **1608** | Samuel de Champlain sails from Normandy to found Québec. |
| **1682** | Cavalier de la Salle of Rouen claims Louisiana for King Louis XIV of France, after sailing down the Mississippi River. |
| **1685** | The Edict of Nantes is revoked; thousands of Protestants involved in business and industry flee Normandy, leaving the area impoverished. |
| **1789–93** | The French Revolution. Thereafter, the province of Normandy ceases to exist, replaced by five *départements*. Turbulent years follow: the Chouans (Royalist Normans) revolt but are crushed. The abbeys are closed, their stones quarried for use elsewhere. |
| **1806** | Sea-bathing becomes 'fashionable'; the coastal resorts begin to develop. Later, the railways accelerate the growth. |
| **1825** | The first regular cross-channel ferry between Normandy and England links Dieppe and Newhaven. |
| **1870** | Franco-Prussian War. Prussian soldiers occupy parts of Normandy and Le Mans. |
| **1872** | Monet paints *Impression: Soleil Levant* at Le Havre and exhibits it in Paris in 1874; the Impressionist movement is born. |
| **1914–18** | World War I. |
| **1939–45** | World War II. France is attacked for the third time in 70 years. The Germans occupy Normandy and many other parts of France. |
| **1944** | 6 June: the D-Day landings in Normandy begin the Liberation of Europe. |
| **1994** | The Pont de Normandie, a 2.1km (1$^1$/2-mile) bridge with a central span of 865m (2,837ft), links Le Havre with the autoroute across the River Seine. |
| **1997** | The Tour de France starts in Rouen to commemorate local hero Jacques Anquetil, five-time winner of the race. |
| **2004** | World heads of state gather in Arromanches to mark the 60th anniversary of the D-Day landings. |

Politics is a serious and passionate business in Normandy and throughout France

# Governance

In the 1980s, the highly centralised government structure in France was reorganised. Power was devolved to the grassroots, though justice, education and health remain national responsibilities. In the next layer down, Basse and Haute Normandy are two of 22 regions, which in turn are subdivided into 96 *départements*. The lowest levels are *communes*, over 36,500 districts, each with a mayor.

## Administration

The regions administer tourism, cultural heritage, industrial development and continuing education; *départements* oversee social services and welfare while the *communes* handle environmental matters, building and planning.

*Départements* have identifying numbers, shown on car licence plates (the last two digits) and used for postcodes: Calvados 14, Eure 27, Manche 50, Orne 61 and Seine-Maritime 76. The regions of Upper and Lower Normandy encompass Eure and Seine-Maritime (Upper), Calvados, Manche and Orne (Lower Normandy).

## Political parties

France has five recognisable political parties. The UMP (Union pour un Mouvement Populaire) is a major player and an heir to the old Gaullist party of General de Gaulle. It encourages privatisation, low taxes and business. The UDF (Union pour la Démocratie Française), right-of-centre, tends to work in coalition with the UMP. The PS (Parti Socialiste) has moved controversially towards the centre (pro-Europe and pro-NATO), while the PCF (Parti Communiste Français) has slumped in popularity since World War II. The party that has received most publicity in recent years is the FN (Front National), the ultra-right-wing racist party founded by Jean-Marie le Pen.

The 2002 presidential elections proved something of a shock for France, when a run-off election pitted Le Pen against the incumbent Chirac (who won with 85 per cent of the vote in Normandy and France).

The 2005 'NON!' for the European constitutional treaty was also a product of the complex world of French party politics – more extreme parties on either end tended to push for no, while those closer to centre (UMP, Socialists) campaigned vainly for a 'oui'.

## The Normans

Overall, Normandy leans to the right when it comes to politics, as the rural vote dominates: the two Conseils Généraux are right-wingers. Even Rouen and Caen have right-leaning councils despite being industrialised. However, three other cities were Communist for decades: Le Havre, Dieppe and Évreux.

# Culture

A century ago, two out of three Normans worked in the fields, and it is all too easy to regard the Normandy of today as one big, happy farmyard. However, with more than 60 per cent of Normans living in towns and only 5 per cent of Normans working as farmers, the rural population is declining. Not that there are many big towns: Caen and Le Havre have populations of about 200,000; Rouen, with 400,000, is the largest city.

Geraniums brighten the stonework on a house in Lassay-les-Châteaux

### A rural tradition

France is one of the world's leading exporters of food. Normandy produces over 10 per cent of the nation's wheat and 10 per cent of its beef. To do this, hedges have been pulled up and fields enlarged to take tractors and harvesters. The European Union demands greater efficiency; the Common Agricultural Policy is not expected to protect the small farmer for much longer. Small, traditional farms are no longer economically viable, and are often bought as secondary residences.

### Food from land and sea

Luckily, Normandy's reputation for farm produce of high quality stands the region in good stead. Ducks and geese, usually associated with southwestern France, are now reared in Normandy too. The demand for *pré-salé* lamb from the salt marshes is being satisfied by ever bigger flocks of sheep along the coast.

The wealth brought to Fécamp and Dieppe by Newfoundland cod may be only a memory, but shellfish production (oysters, mussels, scallops) thrives in several small seaside towns. There are still 1,000 fishing boats and 4,000 fishermen hauling in 70,000 tonnes (68,894 tons) of fish and shellfish every year, often for processing in efficient, modern factory ships. The port of Le Havre is one of Europe's largest, handling 10 per cent of the continent's imports.

### Industry: past, present and future

In the 1950s, Renault and Citroën, Moulinex and Philips built factories in this rural region, close to Paris. The recessions of the '80s and '90s hit these, as well as traditional heavy industries such as steel and shipbuilding, which ceased to be competitive. Tourism is now a major employer, particularly as the hoped-for move to high technology failed to live up to expectations. Power stations produce more electricity than the region needs; the nuclear reprocessing plant at Cap de la Hague is a major employer on the Cotentin Peninsula. Food processing is also a major employer, especially for dairy and meat products.

## Communication links

Communications are improving, with new roads throughout the region and a revitalised railway system linking with the high-speed TGV network and the Channel Tunnel link. There are several convenient cross-Channel ferry routes to England and Ireland, but the charming river ferries (*bacs*) have been superseded by bridges spanning the Seine, notably the 2.1-km (1¹/₂-mile) Pont de Normandie, opened in 1994.

## Changing . . .

Normandy faces big challenges and the revival of urban centres is a priority. After the massive destruction of World War II, speedy rebuilding was necessary but, unfortunately, the results look shabby now. Improvements are being made, with pedestrianised areas,

renovation of old architecture and the embellishment of parks and squares. Although French city-dwellers still love the picture-book Normandy countryside, many are discovering the delights of 'city culture'. Away from the beaches, visitors take a keen interest in watching clogs being made or linen being woven.

## . . . but still Norman

The rest of France considers the Normans to be almost English in their habits: they take great pride in their homes and are famous for their love of gardens and gardening. Towns and villages seem neater and tidier than in the rest of France. As people, 'we may be a little cold at first, but we warm up quickly', says one hotelier, who sees tourism as a vital part of the new Normandy.

Bucolic charm: a traditional half-timbered outbuilding and kitchen garden

# Festivals and events

With its rural and seafaring traditions, it is only natural that most celebrations in Normandy are linked with the fruits of agriculture and the bounty of the sea. Some are modern but others date back hundreds of years. In Granville, for example, the February Carnival started as a farewell celebration for fishermen about to set sail for the Newfoundland Banks.

Medieval style at Crèvecoeur

In Lessay, the Foire Ste-Croix dates back to 1216 and now attracts thousands in September to watch the farmers poke and prod livestock. In Villedieu-les-Poêles, the Grand-Sacré procession commemorates the founding of the town by the Knights of Malta in the 11th century (*June, every four years: 2008, 2012*).

For an up-to-date listing of festivals, fairs and other events, use the Normandy tourist board website: *www.normandy-tourism.org*

**February**
**Granville**
Carnival (*Sunday before Shrove Tuesday*).

**March**
**Mortagne-au-Perche**
Black Pudding Fair (*Mid-month*).

**April**
**Le Mans**
24-hour motorcycle race (*Mid-month*).

**April/May**
**Le Mans**
Europa Jazz Festival at the Abbaye de l'Épau.

**May**
**Coutances**
Jazz Sous les Pommiers (*Ascension weekend*).
**Étretat**
Blessing of the Sea (*Ascension Thursday*); Festival of Normandy (*Ascension weekend*).
**Honfleur**
Sea festival and pilgrimage to the chapel of Notre-Dame-de-Grâce above town (*Whitsun weekend*).
**Lessay**
Mont-St-Michel spring festival (*first Sunday*); St-Thomas Livestock Fair (*first Sunday*).
**Longny-au-Perche**
National tripe competition (*May 1*).
**Pont-l'Évêque**
Cheese Festival (*early May*).
**Rouen**
Joan of Arc Festival (*Sunday nearest May 30*).
**Le Tréport**
Mussel Fair (*late May*).

**June**
**Le Mans**
24-hour sports car race (*mid-month*).

## July
**Château de Balleroy**
Balloon Festival (*first week*).
**Fécamp**
Festival of the Sea (*first weekend*).
**Granville**
Sea Festival (*end of month*).
**Mont-St-Michel**
Beach pilgrimage (*end of month*).

## Mid-July to September
**Fécamp**
Music festival.

## August
**Lisieux**
Procession of the Virgin (*August 15*).
**Livarot**
Town fFestival (*first weekend*).

## September
**Deauville**
Festival of American Films (*beginning of month*).
**Le Havre**
Fishermen's Festival (*beginning of month*).
**Lessay**
Festival of Ste-Croix (*second weekend*).
**Lisieux**
Festival of Ste Thérèse (*last Sunday*).

## October
**Trouville-sur Mer**
Trouville Horse Brocatelle (Equine-themed second-hand market) (*check locally*).

## November
**Dieppe**
Herring Fair (*first Sunday*).
**Rouen**
St-Romain Fair (*first week*).

**Vire:**
Andouille (sausage) Fair (*first weekend*).

## December
**Évreux**
St Nicholas Fair (*December 6*).

Christmas Markets, such as the ones in **Rouen** and **Caen**, are popular across Normandy (*around December 25, check locally for details*).

Feast of the Assumption in Lisieux

Spire of the Benedictine
distillery at Fécamp

# Impressions

*'How came the flame-haired Norsemen to these
lands of fattest pasture and brightest bloom,
fresh-painted daily by a loving, dewy brush?
Bitter, indeed, the north wind that filled their sails.'*

**FEARNE D'ARCY**

Although the inhabitants of the region are proud to trace their ancestry back to the Scandinavians, they are 100 per cent French. The shrug of the shoulders, the gesticulating hands, the familiar body language are all on view. At the same time, there is often a feeling of old-time hospitality, where the foreign visitor is more of a guest than a tourist.

## Man-made Normandy
### Arts Décoratifs (Decorative Arts)
As well as the artists who drew inspiration from Normandy (*see pp34–5*), craftsmen contributed to the cultural heritage of this region. In Dieppe and Fécamp the speciality skill was carving ivory; Alençon, Argentan and Bayeux were renowned throughout Europe for lace until the machines of Nottingham in England put paid to such labour-intensive hand-work. Rouen was a textile centre but it is faïence that merits its own museum there. The tin-glaze on this earthenware provided a sheen for floral patterns and, in the Revolutionary era, political sentiments. Pays d'Auge and salt-glaze pottery are produced from the heavy clay soils, resulting in more rustic wares. As for wood-carving, the *armoire de mariage* (wedding wardrobe) was more than just

a cupboard for clothes: decorated with doves, fruit and flowers, this dowry gift was a work of art.

### Castles
Fortifications abound in Normandy. Around every corner it seems there are souvenirs from the centuries of war: if the Normans were not battling against the English, then they were fighting their neighbours in Maine. These castles served as fortress and bank vault in addition to homes for the powerful administrators of the land.

### Churches, cathedrals and abbeys
What astonishes the observant visitor is the individuality each master mason or architect managed to stamp on the standard cruciform design. Compare the bare simplicity of the church of St-Martin-de-Boscherville and the flamboyant swagger of St-Ouen in Rouen, less than an hour away. Or the elegant technology of the lantern tower on the nave of Coutances Cathedral (Gothic) and the neo-Gothic imitation surmounting the cathedral of Bayeux.

Some have stained-glass windows and tapestries, others delicate stonework and the gilded cups, boxes and regalia that were (and sometimes still are) used in religious ceremonies. Also admire the grotesque carved faces hidden above pillars or among decorative leaves.

## City sophistication

City-lovers enjoy the atmosphere of Rouen, where a modern public transport system sends suburban commuters into the cobblestoned heart of the largest city in Normandy. There are art galleries and concert halls, restaurants and antique shops and the glory of the great cathedral. Shopping is good, too, in Caen which has pedestrianised more of its old streets. Like Rouen and Caen, Le Mans has a university, which contributes to the artistic life and to the energy of the city.

## Half-timbered houses

Think of architecture in Normandy, and you think half-timbered. The Norman farmhouse is the archetype of this style, but in towns and cities, too, streets are lined with 'colombage', as the style is known. Rouen and Domfront have some excellent examples.

The half-timbering of Normandy comes in many colour combinations: brown against ochre, chocolate against pink, grey against white. Sometimes bricks add an extra dimension of pattern. While snug cottages with thatched roofs are classics of this style, surprisingly large houses were also built this way. Bayeux, the Auge region, and even the old quarter of non-Norman Le Mans still have excellent examples of this type (see p73). However, stone plays a significant part in local building, most notably the mellow-coloured stone found around Caen, with stone

buildings more common through western and southern Normandy. Old stone buildings are typified by the round Norman arch, well-known in English church architecture dating from the Norman period.

The *longere* style of house, often just one room deep and with barns abutting at one or both ends, is common in rural areas, but there are houses in much more grand, and typically French, style to be found.

## A variety of villages

From mere hamlets to bustling market centres, these communities are what visitors think of as typically Norman. Some are unattractive, straggling along main roads, so that the inhabitants have to wait for gaps in traffic to cross from the café to the *boulangerie* (bread shop). Others are almost hidden from view, tucked away in small valleys. The prettiest, such as St-Fraimbault in the Orne, are rated for their flowers, in gardens or window boxes. Many, like Bricquebec on the Cotentin Peninsula and Chambois near Argentan, have huge impressive *donjons* (keeps).

## Natural Normandy

Pick up a large-scale map and lose yourself in the spider's web of tiny roads

### World War II

Much of Normandy was devastated by bombing, particularly before D-Day and then during the Battle of Normandy in the summer of 1944. The 50th anniversary of that invasion provided impetus for improving the displays and smartening up the image of many of the museums and monuments (see pp66–9).

in the *bocage*, the tiny meadows with high hedges. Some have no signposts, and you could end up in a farmyard or back where you started. All are well paved even if narrow; single-track roads have passing places for cars and tractors. Travel by car and you travel too fast; travel by foot and you appreciate just how large Normandy is. Travel by bicycle, however, and you have the best of both worlds. On a *vélo* you can see over hedges, quickly find shelter in a sudden shower and work up an appetite.

### Beaches

Normandy does not have the blistering heat of the Mediterranean, but that can be an advantage for families with small children. Certainly, there is plenty of sand for building castles, rock pools for discovering shrimp and seaweed to smell. Old blends with new: traditional beach huts still stand in a line while teenagers slice through the water on surfboards.

### Cliffs

Not all of the Normandy coastline is flat sand. Chalk cliffs have been weathered

Gentle greens and gentle slopes provide the themes for many Normandy landscapes

Normans can seem taciturn, but most will treat visitors as welcome guests

into doorways at Étretat, but could have been sawn off by a giant near Dieppe. The Pointe du Hoc (*see p67*) posed a stern challenge for the invasion forces on D-Day, while on the northwestern tip of the Cotentin Peninsula, drivers must take care not to be distracted by dramatic views as backroads suddenly twist or drop steeply downhill.

### The seasons

In spring, Normandy's orchards explode into a snowstorm of apple blossom while hedges are spotted with wild flowers. In summer, caravan parks and campsites fill with holiday-makers and the chic head for Deauville. Piles of yellowy-red apples fill orchards and the acid smell cuts through the autumn air as the fruit is crushed to make cider and calvados. As the leaves fall, country houses and mansions are no longer hidden from view. Dampness lends an extra chill to the air, and famous cathedrals and abbeys are as inviting as refrigerators, though at least the camera-toting hordes of summer have departed. Nowhere is worth a winter visit more than Mont-St-Michel. Photographers can sleep late and still snap the dawn light shining on the mount, while at night only a few people bother to walk the ramparts and explore the alleys which, without the crowds, are full of medieval atmosphere.

### The people

The best place to strike up a conversation – as long as there is no impatient queue behind you – is in a food shop. Ask about the breads, and the flour-dusted baker himself may appear to point out his special six-grain bread or country loaf. Show interest in a *charcuterie* (delicatessen) and you may be given a taste of *pâté* and *rillette* or advice on what to buy for a picnic. Talk to a *fromager* and you could be discussing and comparing cheeses for hours. The Normans love their food, are proud of their food and talk a lot about it.

### Thomas Cook's Normandy

Cook started trips to the French coast in 1865, visiting Honfleur, Caen, Cherbourg, St Malo and other places 'of great historical interest to enlightened British travellers'. In 1882, John Mason Cook (Thomas's son) visited Normandy with a view to making arrangements for a new tour. In 1896, a personally conducted cycling tour of Normandy was advertised. Normandy grew to be a particularly popular seaside destination for British tourists in the 1930s, '40s and '50s.

Huge, nearly empty, sandy beaches like this one north of Carteret are the best-kept secrets on the Cotentin Peninsula

# Northeastern Normandy

Paris traditionally had two routes to the English Channel: overland to Dieppe, the nearest port, or via the River Seine. Between the two lies the flat Caux (chalk) plateau, broken by the wooded region of Bray and the beautiful beech forest of Lyons.

Colourful view of Dieppe's Grand Rue

The importance of the River Seine was summed up by Napoleon: 'Le Havre, Rouen and Paris are but a single town of which the Seine is the main street.' Although this is a busy thoroughfare, there are idyllic orchards, pretty villages and brooding castles on its banks. At the mouth of the river, Le Havre 'the Harbour' was built; Caudebec-en-Caux and Rouen were ports first developed for sailing ships, then for steam-powered vessels.

This area of Normandy is full of history. Back in 1050, Duke William of Normandy persuaded Mathilda of Flanders to marry him at the border of their territories, the castle of Eu. This

was replaced by a 16th-century château (now the Town Hall), which was lavishly redecorated by King Louis-Philippe 250 years later. On the coast, Fécamp and Dieppe were departure points for explorers claiming land and merchants buying goods for France.

**Architectural heritage and the arts**

Northeastern Normandy has plenty of variety and interest for the visitor beyond the spectacular coastal scenery of the towering chalk cliffs at Étretat, including museums, religious and military ruins, and the ancient city of Rouen with its magnificent cathedral, a monument to early engineers. Then there is Lyons-la-

There are two natural arches on the cliffs at Étretat; this one is the Falaise d'Aval

## Northeastern Normandy

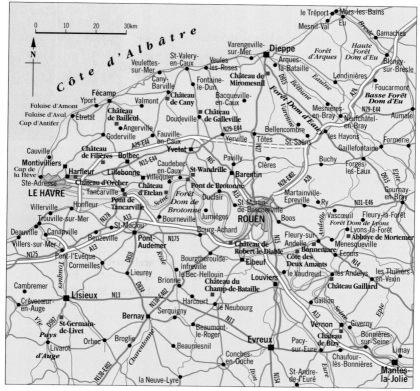

Forêt, a well-preserved village full of half-timbered houses, which is a touring centre for the surrounding woodlands. In medieval times, the lush water-meadows and mild climate of the Seine valley attracted monks who built some of the great abbeys of Europe: Jumièges, St-Wandrille and St-Martin-de-Boscherville.

The garden and ponds at Giverny modelled for some of Claude Monet's best-known paintings, and further down the River Seine, at Villequier, a family tragedy inspired the heart-rending

poetry of Victor Hugo whose house, like Monet's, is a shrine to enthusiasts. Flaubert based his notorious novel *Madame Bovary* on Ry, which is now the centre of a 'Madame Bovary' tourist industry. Another writer, Guy de Maupassant, spent his formative years in the Château de Miromesnil, near Dieppe, which perhaps triggered his jaundiced view of bourgeois society. Contemporary art is not forgotten: the 16th-century Château de Vascoeuil holds audacious displays of modern sculpture, paintings and crafts.

# Rouen

Joan of Arc burned at the stake; the cathedral, painted by Impressionist Claude Monet; the Gros Horloge, the 16th-century clock in the old quarter: Rouen is different things to different people. The modern city sprawls along the banks of the River Seine, an unattractive muddle of docks and warehouses halfway between Paris and the sea. Its suburbs spread south to fill a huge bend in the river, while the bright new university campus covers a hilltop to the north.

The lantern tower of St-Ouen's church soars over the rue de Miette

In Roman times, **Rotomagus** was a major administrative centre in Gaul. Later, Rollo the Viking, the first Duke of Normandy, dredged the river, built embankments and established a city that became the capital of Haute Normandie (Upper Normandy) and now the capital of the *département* of Seine-Maritime. Once the English were finally expelled in the 15th century, Rouen enjoyed a golden age, fired by the enthusiasm of Cardinal Georges of Amboise who introduced Italian-influenced architecture. The extravagant Palais de Justice (law courts) is one legacy of the 16th century, when explorers and merchants sailed up the River Seine from Dieppe, Honfleur and Le Havre. The prosperity of the 17th century is exemplified by mansions such as the Hôtel d'Hocqueville, now the ceramics museum dedicated to faïence, the French version of majolica, a tin-glazed earthenware.

Weaving was an important industry, though this suffered from the revocation

Beautifully maintained houses help to make Rouen one of France's most attractive cities

of the Edict of Nantes (1685), which prompted the Huguenot (Protestant) traders and businessmen to flee, taking their technical know-how abroad. As ever, Rouen recovered and in the 18th century its textile industry added *rouennerie*, a coarse, blue printed cotton fabric to its repertoire; then came twill and velveteen. The city's docks thrived, virtually becoming a warehouse for Paris, and ranked among France's five largest ports, as they still do today.

In World War II, the Allies bombed the port and bridges, unfortunately badly damaging the strip between the river and the cathedral. The most

important buildings were reconstructed and today Rouen looks lively with its high-quality shops. Wander from '*clocher en clocher*' (spire to spire) through the 6km (3½ miles) of pedestrianised streets in the old town (*see pp32–3*); discover the bust of Impressionist Claude Monet in the place St-Amand; and explore the Quartier St-Maclou, with its antique shops and the delightful rue de Robec, where half-timbered houses have tiny bridges across the small stream. Rouen is proud of its public transport system, while riverside areas are being cleaned up and redeveloped for housing.

## Rouen (*see p32 for orange route walk*)

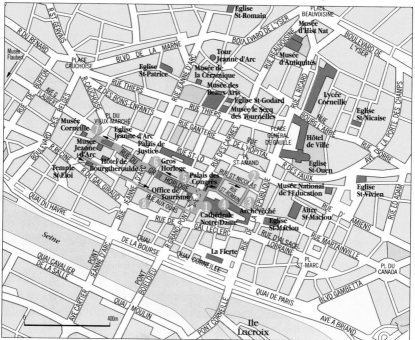

Rouen has many fascinating old buildings; the Gros-Horloge is particularly fine

## Aître St-Maclou

The carved skulls, bones and shovels in the timber beams in this peaceful quadrangle are evidence that this was a warehouse for the bones of plague victims four centuries ago. It is now the École des Beaux-Arts, the art college.
*186 rue Martainville. Open: daily, standard hours (see pp186–7). Free admission.*

## Beffroi du Gros-Horloge

Six centuries old, the Great Clock still tells the time with a single hand, the day of the week indicated by the planets and phases of the moon (*see p33*). The medieval mechanism is in the recently renovated belfry where the Cache-Ribaud bell still rings the curfew at 9pm, as it has since 1260. The clocktower is scheduled to reopen in 2007 following a painstaking 15-year restoration project, but it's still lovely from the outside.
*Rue du Gros-Horloge. Tel: 02 35 71 28 40. Open: Palm Sunday–Sept, Wed–Mon. Closed: Tue & Wed mornings. Admission charge.*

Intimations of mortality on Aître St-Maclou, a former charnel house

When La Pucelle d'Orléans, the Maid of Orleans, was born a simple peasant girl in Lorraine in 1412, France was in disarray. The English and the Dukes of Burgundy controlled more territory than the crown; then, in the Battle of Agincourt (1415), King Henry V of England routed the French and retook Normandy. Charles VII, who succeeded to the French throne in 1422, remained uncrowned seven years later.

When visions of saints told the teenage Joan to rescue her country, few believed her, but she did not give up and eventually gained an audience with the king. He disguised himself in an attempt to trick her, but Joan was

not fooled and persuaded him to allow her to lead an attack on the English at Orléans. Dressed in armour, she rallied the demoralised French and led them to a shock victory. The coronation of King Charles VII followed.

A year later she was captured by the Burgundians who sold her to the English.

Joan's trial of heresy and sorcery was held in Rouen, which was still controlled by the English. Threatened with torture and death, she recanted, denying her visions and was sentenced to life imprisonment. The story goes that Joan had to promise not to wear men's clothes, but when she had to leave her cell for 'bodily necessities' only men's clothes were available. Caught 'breaking her oath', she was sentenced to death.

On 30 May 1431, just 19 years old, she was burnt at the stake in the old market place. An ecclesiastical tribunal declared the trial illegal in 1456; 464 years later, in 1920, Joan was canonised. In World War II, the cross of Lorraine from Joan's native province was the symbol of the Free French.

Above: sculpture depicting Joan preparing for death at the memorial site in Rouen
Left: Joan of Arc's execution spot in Rouen's place du Vieux Marché

## Cathédrale Notre-Dame

Renovation work on the cathedral, part of a continuing process, has exposed the creamy-white stone of the west front and highlighted the montage of Gothic styles. The St-Romain tower on the left rises from 12th-century simplicity to 15th-century complexity and houses a 9.5-tonne bell called the Jeanne d'Arc. On the right, the Tour de Beurre, six layers of flamboyant stonework capped by an octagonal crown, has a 56-bell carillon. Soaring 151m (495 ft) is l'Aigle, the highest spire in France, topped by a red copper cockerel weighing 17kg (37 pounds – 'the size of a sheep'). The changing light on this front was captured by Claude Monet in his series of 30 paintings (1892–4).

In the south ambulatory lies the stone effigy of Rollo, first Duke of Normandy, his robe drawn up under his arm. Nearby are his son, William Longsword, and King Richard I of England. While façade restoration is underway, visitors can see some of the exterior niche saints up close, on exhibit around the ambulatory as well. Nothing, however, matches the 16th-century tomb of the Cardinals of Amboise in the Lady Chapel. They kneel humbly but are dressed in rich robes and surrounded by splendid carving. Light pours in through the lantern tower above the altar and stained-glass windows. On the north side, the 13th-century legend of St Julian the Hospitaller reads like a strip cartoon, from bottom to top. Tradition says this inspired Flaubert to write his story about St Julian. Certainly, the cathedral provides a romantic setting for the lovers in his novel *Madame Bovary*.

Intricate stone carving at the entrance to Rouen cathedral

### GUSTAVE FLAUBERT (NOVELIST) 1821–80

Flaubert would sometimes spend days writing just one page; no wonder it took him five years to write *Madame Bovary* (1857), his tale of a bored country wife in search of excitement. Charles and Emma Bovary were based on real people: Eugène Delamare, a Rouen surgeon who studied under Flaubert's father, and his second wife, Delphine Couturier, who had several affairs, then committed suicide. Some aspects of Emma's character are also attributed to the poet Louise Colet, Flaubert's mistress. He lived for most of his life at Croisset, near Rouen, and enjoyed popping the bourgeois bubbles of complacency and respectability.

Photographs on the south side show how bombs disembowelled the cathedral on 19 April 1944. Luckily, two flying buttresses held, preventing the whole nave from collapsing.

*Place de la Cathédrale; www.cathedrale-rouen.net. Open: daily, standard hours (see pp186–7).*

## Église St-Maclou

Photographs inside show how World War II bombs all but flattened this fine example of flamboyant Gothic architecture. The west front is crowned with a lacy, stonework tiara, while below, five 15th-century portals – and modern pigeons – greet visitors. The three central doors portray a sobering vision of the *Last Judgement*, though much of the carving needs renovation, as does the rest of the church, which only reopened in 1980.

*Place Barthélémy. Open: daily. Closed: Sun morning.*

## Église St-Ouen

This former Benedictine abbey church is a breathtaking example of Gothic airiness and light, built to house the remains of St Ouen, a 7th-century Bishop of Rouen. Begun in 1318, it owes the continuity of Gothic style to Alexandre and Colin de Berneval, father and son, who strictly followed the plans of the abbot, Jean Roussel. Music lovers can enjoy the 19th-century Cavaillé-Coll organ.

*Place Général de Gaulle. Open: summer, daily; winter, Wed, Sat & Sun. Closed: Tue & mid-Dec–mid-Jan. Free admission.*

## Musée des Beaux-Arts (Museum of Fine Arts)

This museum is worth a visit just to see one of Monet's famous studies of Rouen Cathedral among the Impressionist works and Old Master paintings. One of 15 national museums set up in 1801, their international collections are especially strong in the 19th century. Don't miss the chance to see works by the artists of Normandy's golden age of inspiration – their Impressionist collection includes Monet's cathedral studies, Dufy's fresh views of the seaside, and native sons such as Boudin.

*Place Verdrel. Tel: 02 35 71 28 40; www.rouen-musees.com. Open: daily, standard hours (see pp186–7). Closed: Tue. Admission charge.*

The breathtaking artistry and technical skill of medieval masons on display at St-Maclou

## Musée de la Céramique (Ceramics Museum)

Strictly for fans of porcelain, this collection of Rouen faïence is housed in the 17th-century Hôtel d'Hocqueville. In Room 15, '*Vivre libre ou mourir*' ('Live free or die') is just one of the uplifting messages on plates, bowls and jugs from the Revolutionary period.
*1 rue Faucon. Tel: 02 35 07 31 74. Open: daily, except Tue. Admission charge.*

## Musée Flaubert et Musée d'Histoire de la Medécine (Flaubert Birthplace and Museum of the History of Medicine)

In 1821, author Gustave Flaubert was born in this mansion, next to the Hôtel-Dieu (hospital). His father was a surgeon, so alongside medical implements are Flaubert memorabilia, including his famous (stuffed) parrot.
*51 rue Lecat.*
*Tel: 02 35 15 59 95.*
*http://trouveur.chu-rouen.fr/museeflaubert/sommaire.htm. Open: Tue–Sat, standard hours (see pp186–7), may be closed occasional Saturdays for events. Admission charge.*

## Musée le Secq des Tournelles (Wrought-iron Museum)

Intriguing locks on coffers, a complete banister and hundreds of keys are among 12,000 items installed in an old church.
*Rue Jacques Villon.*
*Tel: 02 35 88 42 92.*
*Open: Wed–Mon, standard hours (see pp186–7).*
*Admission charge.*

## Palais de Justice (Law Courts)

Built in 1499 as a merchant's hall, and seat of the Normandy Parliament from 1514, this sports fancy Gothic stonework that looks like the inspiration for London's Houses of Parliament. The façade on Place Foch retains its World War II pockmarks – a rare memento in this meticulously restored quarter. Contact the Rouen tourist office for scheduled tours of the interior to see the left wing where Pierre Corneille, the dramatist-lawyer, would have climbed the vast staircase to the Salle des Procureurs or des Pas Perdus, an ancient courtroom. An 850-year-old Jewish structure was excavated under the cobblestones of the main

## PIERRE CORNEILLE (DRAMATIST) 1606–84

Rouen-born Corneille's early works were tales of love and comedy, but, summoned to Paris by Cardinal Richelieu, he changed direction. With *Le Cid* in 1636, he began creating larger-than-life heroes and heroines forced to choose between honour and passion. Where Greek tragedians bemoaned man's inability to alter fate, Corneille argued that man could make his own destiny. Parisian theatre-goers loved his work, though Richelieu discouraged the playwright. But Corneille continued to write, in his country home south of Rouen (*see p31*), breaking new ground for play-wrights such as Racine who followed, and earning the title 'founder of French classical drama'.

courtyard in 1976 and can also be visited.
*Rue aux Juifs.*

## Place du Vieux Marché

Dominating the old market square is the sweeping modern church dedicated to Joan of Arc, who was burnt at the stake here in 1431. A 20-m (66-ft) high cross marks the spot. Many original half-timbered buildings survive: some are restaurants, such as La Couronne, claiming to be the oldest *auberge* (inn) in France. Next door, the Musée Jeanne d'Arc is a depressingly touristy waxwork summary of the saint's life and times.
*Tel: 02 35 88 02 70; www.jeanne-darc.com. Open: daily. Admission charge.*

## Tour Jeanne d'Arc

This tower with 4-m (13-ft) thick walls is the sole survivor of a 12th-century castle. Alas, it's unlikely that Joan of Arc spent much time in this tower, as is often rumoured, but its exhibits on medieval life are themselves worth the stairs. Climb 50 steps for the history of the castle, 37 more for a history of the area; a further 35 to the top.
*Rue du Donjon. Tel: 02 35 98 16 21. Open: daily. Closed: Tue & Sun, mornings. Admission charge.*

## Nearby
### Château de Martainville

As well as housing a comprehensive review of Norman furniture and architecture, this 15th-century mansion has fine examples of jewellery and pottery, costumes and glass, with a typical farmhouse interior.
*16km (10 miles) east of Rouen.*

*Tel: 02 35 23 44 70. Open: daily, except Tue & Sun, mornings. Admission charge.*

## Maison des Champs de Pierre Corneille

Although the dramatist would feel at home with the furniture and books inside his country retreat, he would be horrified by the factories and suburbs that have come up around this 17th-century, half-timbered house.
*8km (5 miles) south of Rouen. 502 rue Pierre Corneille, Petit-Couronne. Tel: 02 35 68 13 89. Open: Wed–Mon, standard hours (see pp186–7). Closed: Nov. Admission charge.*

## Pavillon et Musée Flaubert

Flaubert was a perfectionist. He would walk under the lime trees repeating sentences from *Madame Bovary*, which he wrote in this riverside house. One wing remains, filled with mementoes.
*Canteleu, Dieppedalle-Croiset. 18 quai Gustave Flaubert, 5km (3 miles) west of Rouen. Tel: 02 35 71 28 82. Open: Wed afternoon–Mon, standard hours (see pp186–7). Admission charge.*

Place du Vieux Marché, Rouen: traditional market and new church dedicated to St Joan

# Walk: Old Rouen

Walking is the only way to appreciate the medieval buildings and tiny alleyways that survived World War II bomb damage.

*See map on page 25 for route.*

*Allow one hour.*

*Start in place de la Cathédrale where the tourist office began in 1509 as the Bureau des Finances (Exchequer).*

*Note the striking Art Nouveau pharmacy façade next door.*

## 1 Cathédrale Notre-Dame

The west front was often painted by Claude Monet. The central doorway was built by Roulland le Roux. On the left, the St-Romain tower is the oldest part of the cathedral; the Tour de Beurre (Butter Tower) on the right was paid for by dispensations from townspeople desperate to have butter and milk during Lent. (*See p28.*)

*Turn left and cut through rue Georges Lanfry to rue de la Croix-de-Fer. Turn right on rue Saint-Nicolas.*

## 2 Rue Saint-Nicolas

This narrow street of half-timbered houses is a delight for modern shoppers searching for clothes and antiques, toys and jewellery. Look through the doorways to look into ancient courtyards.

*Just past rue St-Amand, turn right into an alleyway – this is the rue des Chanoines.*

## 3 Rue des Chanoines

Barely two people wide, this passageway of dark corners and buckling walls evokes medieval Rouen. The backs of buildings reveal layers of architectural history in wood, stone and slate shingles. High above soar the spires of the cathedral.

*Turn right on to rue Saint-Romain.*

The tomb of the two Cardinals Amboise in the Lady Chapel of Rouen Cathedral

## 4 Rue Saint-Romain

On the Archevêché (Archbishop's Palace), one plaque recalls the trial of Joan of Arc in May 1431, another her rehabilitation by Cardinal d'Estouteville 25 years later. Admire No 74, a classic 15th-century house with a lion's head on the door, carved figures and leaded glass windows.

*Return to place de la Cathédrale. Cross the cathedral square and walk down the pedestrianised rue du Gros-Horloge.*

## 5 Rue du Gros-Horloge

Look above chain-store windows to appreciate the age of the houses. At the corner of rue du Bec, a plaque honours Cavalier de la Salle, who explored the Mississippi River and claimed Louisiana for France. Another plaque, on the old Town Hall (corner of rue Thouret), cites M Thouret, a *député* (representative) of Rouen. The date is *14 brumaire an II*. In the Republican calendar introduced after the Revolution, *brumaire* was the second month of the year; the Year II was 1793.

*Continue to Gros-Horloge.*

## 6 Gros-Horloge

In 1527, locals had this highly decorated clock lowered from the next-door belfry so they could see the single hour-hand and phases of the moon more clearly (*see p26*).

*Cross rue Jeanne d'Arc and continue towards the market square.*

## 7 Place du Vieux Marché

A tall cross, *la Croix de la Réhabilitation*, marks the spot where Jeanne d'Arc died (*see p27 & p31*). Today, small restaurants

Filigree stonework and weathered statues on the façade of Rouen Cathedral

occupy the old buildings overlooking a stark, modern church whose design echoes a ship's hull.

*Turn left on rue du Vieux-Palais, then left on rue Samuel Boshart. Cross the square to rue aux Ours.*

## 8 Rue aux Ours

This quiet street has a mixture of architectural styles. Note the medieval house by the ruined St Pierre du Chatel. No 61 was the birthplace of François-Adrian Boïeldieu (1775–1834), composer of operas (*Le Calife de Bagdad* and *La Dame Blanche*). No 46 was the birthplace (1785) of scientist Pierre Louis Dulong, whose research into heat resulted in Dulong and Petit's Law.

*Return to the cathedral.*

# Artists and writers

Over the centuries, Normandy has produced and attracted artists, writers and musicians. Many are national figures; others, such as Boudin (*see p78*), Corneille (*see p30*), Flaubert (*see p28*), de Maupassant (*see p50*) and Monet (*see p48*), have international reputations.

## WRITERS

### Canon Wace of Bayeux (1120–83)

Canon Wace was the first writer to use everyday French. His *Roman de Brut* reinforced the legend of King Arthur, while the *Roman de Rou* described early Norman history.

### Alexandre de Bernay (11th century)

This wandering troubadour, whose poem about Alexander the Great (1,952 lines long) followed a 12-syllable line metre, gave rise to the 'alexandrine' verse metre used centuries later by Corneille and Racine.

### Victor Hugo (1802–85)

France's greatest 19th-century poet spent many years in Normandy and fought for the region when he was in parliament. The 1980s' hit musical, *Les Misérables*, was adapted from his book; his moving poem, *A Villequier*, was inspired by the death of his daughter (*see p37*).

### Alexis de Tocqueville (1805–59)

De Tocqueville, a brilliant politician from the Cotentin peninsula, is remembered for his incisive analysis of democracy in America and the French Revolution.

### Marcel Proust (1871–1922)

Having spent childhood holidays in Cabourg, Proust wrote about Normandy in many of his award-winning novels. Cabourg, for example, is the Balbec of *À l'Ombre des Jeunes Filles en Fleurs*.

## ARTISTS

In addition to Monet and Boudin, Renoir, Seurat, Pissarro and Sisley also painted profusely in Normandy, known as the birthplace of Impressionism, at Honfleur and Le Havre.

### Jean-François Millet (1814–75)

The Norman countryside often features in landscapes by this son of a peasant from the Cotentin peninsula. Sentimental scenes like *Les Glaneuses* (The Gleaners) make popular living-room prints today, but he was condemned as a 'socialist' in his later years.

### Fernand Léger (1881–1955)

From the same peasant background as Millet, the innovative Cubist has a surprisingly low profile in his home town of Argentan. Near Lisores, his farmhouse sports a boldly coloured mural of a milkmaid and cow.

Facing page: bust of the writer Proust, in the foyer of the Grand Hôtel in Cabourg
Below: Monet's house at Giverny

# Tour: the banks of the Seine

The River Seine has long been a major transport route. This drive traces a quiet loop, where industry is absent but there is history behind every wall.

*The tour starts in Rouen. Allow half a day.*

*Leave Rouen on the D982, following signs for Canteleu. The road affords spectacular views over the River Seine. At St-Martin-de-Boscherville, turn left to the Abbaye St-Georges.*

## 1 St-Martin-de-Boscherville

Such a massive abbey in so small a village is a surprise (*see p52*). Careful restoration is returning the massive walls of the abbey to its 11th-century glory.

*Return to the D982, following signs for Jumièges and Duclair.*

## 2 Duclair

After driving through orchards and past ancient barns, the River Seine reappears

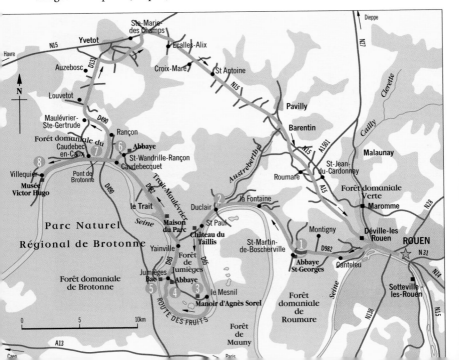

on the left. Enter the Parc Naturel Régional de Brotonne and the straggling hamlet of Duclair, known for its ducks. Here the *bac* (ferry) takes cars and foot passengers 100m (328 ft) across the river.
*Just beyond Duclair, turn left on to the D65 towards le Mesnil.*

### 3  Le Mesnil
Spot the garages built into the cliff behind thatched cottages. Gnarled trees in orchards produce Melrose, Jonagold and Golden Delicious apples. Le Monde Merveilleux des Abeilles (The Wonderful World of Bees, *tel: 02 35 91 36 76*) is a small apiculture farm outside Mesnil, known for its 700-year-old manor house where Agnès Sorel, the influential mistress of Charles VII, died in 1450, aged 28.
*Continue towards Jumièges on the Route des Fruits.*

### 4  Jumièges
A high stone wall on the right announces Jumièges. The twin towers of the 7th-century Benedictine abbey (*see p50*) still dwarf the houses at its gate. Legend recalls the *énervés*, the princes whose hamstrings were cut in punishment for rebelling against Queen Bathilde in the 7th century and who sought asylum here.

### 5  Bac
If there is time, drive down to the *bac* landing station where a small *auberge* is a peaceful spot for refreshment while admiring the cliffs across the Seine.
*Return to the main road, which rejoins the D982. Turn left towards le Trait, but once the Pont de Brotonne (Brotonne Bridge) comes into view, watch carefully for the sign to St-Wandrille on the right, the D22.*

### 6  St-Wandrille
The huge, ornate, wrought-iron gate leads to an abbey (*see p52*). Outside the walls is the village church which dates from the 11th century.
*Return to the D982 and turn right for Caudebec.*

### 7  Caudebec-en-Caux
On the right, almost in the shadow of the Pont de Brotonne, stands a monument to five brave, near-forgotten aviators – Guilbaud, de Cuverville, Dietrichson, Brazy and Valette. In 1928 they flew to the Arctic Circle to rescue Italian balloonists who had crashed near Spitzbergen. The Frenchmen and the Norwegian explorer Amundsen were lost without trace in their Latham 47, built at the still functioning aero factory nearby. Away from the main road, the attractive heart of Caudebec centres on the medieval church of Notre-Dame and the Maison des Templiers (*see p39*).
*Continue on the D982; fork left to Villequier, beyond Caudebec.*

### 8  Villequier
Houses crowd the bank in this attractive village, which is synonymous with author Victor Hugo (*see p34*). In a riverside park just before the hamlet, Hugo's statue looks out sadly towards the spot where his daughter and son-in-law were drowned by the infamous *mascaret* (tidal bore) in 1843.
*Turn round; return to Rouen via Caudebec, Yvetot and the N15.*

Petit Andely and the River Seine as seen from Château Gaillard

## Les Andelys

The villages of Grand and Petit Andely boast royal and artistic connections. In peaceful Petit Andely, half-timbered houses face the church of St-Sauveur, constructed by King Richard I of England at the end of the 12th century. It survived the Revolution as a store-house for iron and lead. Now its 17th-century organ draws music lovers.

Further up the Gambon River is much busier Grand Andely, with its banks, shops and market. A memorial fountain marks the place where, according to legend, Queen Clothilde turned water into wine for labourers building a monastery in the 6th century. The elegant Notre-Dame church can be compared to Rouen Cathedral, albeit in miniature. Note the scenes of rural life sculpted round the stained-glass windows (1540 and 1560) on the north side of the nave and the three paintings by the unknown Quentin Varin. His pupil was the famous 17th-century artist Nicolas Poussin whose *Coriolanus* hangs in a small museum nearby.

*Musée N Poussin, rue Ste-Clotilde.*
*Tel: 02 32 54 31 78. Open: Wed–Mon, afternoons. Admission charge.*

## Château Gaillard

Just above Petit Andely and dominating this curve of the River Seine is Château Gaillard. Built in one year (1196) at the command of King Richard the Lionheart of England, the combination of fort and moated redoubt set upon a cliff seemed impenetrable. However, in 1204, King Phillipe-Auguste's men filled the outer moat, blew up a tower and then scrambled into the inner courtyard through the lavatory outlets.

*Tel: 02 32 54 04 16. Open: Wed afternoon–Mon, standard hours (see*

Even in ruins Château Gaillard dominates its surroundings

*pp186–7). Closed: mid-Nov–mid-Mar. Admission charge.*

*Les Andelys is 38km (24 miles) southeast of Rouen, on the north bank of the Seine, on the D313.*

### Arques-la-Bataille
The battle of this name took place here in 1589 during the Religious Wars: Henry IV overcame the greater forces of the Catholic Duke of Mayenne, when fog delayed action, allowing the king's superior cannons to gain victory. The hilltop castle's inner gate bears a carved record of the success. The fortifications date back to 1038.
*8km (5 miles) southeast of Dieppe.*

### Caudebec-en-Caux
For four centuries Caudebec was the capital of the Caux (Chalk) region that fans out from Rouen to the coast (*see p22*). A popular stopover for pilots navigating boats up the River Seine, the town was regularly flooded by the *mascaret* (tidal bore) until this was tamed in 1965. All this is explained in the **Musée de la Marine de Seine**, where an old notice board outside still records the day's traffic on the river. A fire in 1940 left little of the old town except for some of the 14th-century fortifications, the **Maison des Templiers**, a rare example of a 13th-century private house, and the **Church of Notre-Dame**. Stained-glass windows depicting St George and the coat of arms of one Fulke Eyton are a reminder of the English occupation for 30 of the church's 100 years of construction. There is a lively Saturday market and, on Sunday afternoons, free

Cranes are among the creatures that roam free at the Château de Clères

organ recitals in the church.
*35km (22 miles) northwest of Rouen, on the north bank of the Seine, on the D982. Musée de la Marine de Seine, Avenue Winston Churchill. Tel. 02 35 95 90 13. Open: daily, afternoons, standard hours (see pp186–7). Admission charge.*

### Château de Clères
Clères means just one thing to French families – the zoo. Set in the pretty Clèrette Valley, the 16th-century château on the edge of the village has provided a spectacular setting for wildlife since 1920. A variety of birds and mammals roams free in the parkland, from kangaroos to antelopes and cranes.
*Parc Zoologique. Tel: 02 35 33 23 08. Open: daily, standard hours (see pp186–7). Closed: Dec–mid-Mar. Admission charge.*

*Château de Clères is 16km (10 miles) north of Rouen, off the N27.*

Signs for *l'abbaye de* . . . . appear in towns, villages and on lonely country roads throughout Normandy. Most of these monasteries are in ruins, yet, literally and figuratively, they were the foundation stones of Norman culture and power. The Benedictine monks who set up these communities over 1,000 years ago followed a disciplined creed: *Laborare est orare*, 'to work is to pray'.

Over the years, they developed medicine and mathematics, music and animal husbandry; they drained marshes and tamed forests. Where we have schools and hospitals, libraries and pioneers of industry, Normandy had monasteries and monks.

These establishments were at the heart of cultural life. Thanks to murals and carvings, we can see how the people dressed. With their ability to write, the monks were an invaluable component of the communication network, often carrying messages from one lord to another. In an unstable world they provided organisation, but the wealth of the early settlements led to greed and many were plundered by the Vikings. William the Conqueror revived the power of the Church, using it as an arm of the government; his closest adviser was Lanfranc, a former prior of le Bec-Hellouin. The monasteries, with a new spirit of discipline, grew in power and influence.

The heart of monastic building was the garth or quadrangle, with a herb garden, important both for cooking and for making medicines. Surrounding this were the cloisters, a covered walkway joining all the buildings. On the north side was the abbey church; opposite, the refectory or dining room with a stone basin of water by the door for the monks to wash their hands before eating. On the west side would have been the lay-brothers' (the 'junior'

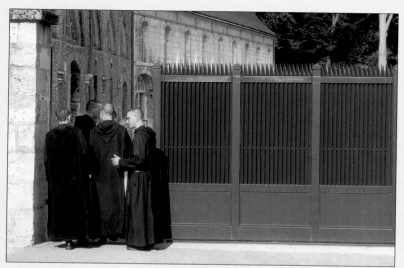

monks') quarters. To the east, between the church and the refectory were meeting rooms: the chapter house, the warming room and the day room. Above was the open dormitory shared by the monks. Outside, gardens and orchards were surrounded by a high wall for privacy and peace.

The outlines of many of these can be seen clearly today: at Jumièges and Hambye, St-Wandrille and le Bec-Hellouin. Sadly, after the monks were evicted during the French Revolution, many buildings were sold off as ready-made stone quarries. But their magnificence and their contribution to Western culture cannot be dismantled.

Today's monasteries are very much part of community life. Although direct contact with the public is eschewed by the strictly governed monastic orders, most contribute to the local economy. The Benedictine liqueur from Fécamp and the biscuits from the Abbey at Lonlaye are well-known throughout France and wider afield, but images of monks toiling away to produce these products are wide off the mark. Factories providing jobs for local people have been set up, and modern business and marketing methods are employed.

Some religious establishments attract tourists to view their spectacular architecture and locations, others provide havens of tranquillity.

Benedictine monks still inhabit part of St-Wandrille Abbey, whose grand ruins reflect the power of the Norman culture at its founding

# Dieppe

A dramatic facelift is improving this port, once badly run-down but now aiming to be a 'little Honfleur'. In 1994, a new terminal diverted ferry-bound cars and lorries from the Avant-port, now converted into a yacht marina. Having renovated the old Quartier St Jacques, the programme now includes the Bout du Quai (end of the quay), another warren of tiny lanes. Traffic-free streets such as the Grande Rue bustle with shoppers, while cafés are extending on to the quayside. Behind the 2km (1¹/₄ miles) of beach are tennis courts, a thalassotherapy centre, and lawns where an international kite-flying competition is held in even-numbered years in September.

Dieppe derives from the Viking word for 'deep', and for centuries this harbour was fought over by the French and English; the latter built the 12th-century castle but were finally ejected three centuries later. The 16th century saw Dieppe become a major port, with a population of 60,000, nearly twice that of today. Relays of horses rushed fish to Paris every night. Privateers captured booty in the Channel and eastern Atlantic; their captain, Jehan Ango (or Jean Ango) is commemorated all over town. His fleet broke Portugal's control of routes round West Africa, allowing Dieppe traders to bring back spices and ivory carved by local craftsmen.

In 1694 the Anglo-Dutch fleet razed the town, ironically, the home of Abraham Duquesne, chief of the French navy. As a Protestant, he could not be given the title of 'Admiral' but he does have a statue in the Place Nationale.

During the French Revolution, English skippers ferried aristocrats and clerics to safety; then, in the 19th century, Dieppe flourished as a holiday resort. French and British holiday-makers arrived by train and the regular ferry service was established in 1825. Lord Salisbury, the Foreign Secretary and later Prime

## THE BLOODY REHEARSAL

On 19 August 1942, some 7,000 troops, mostly Canadian, raided Dieppe. 'Operation Jubilee' was a disaster, with over 1,000 Canadians and 113 RAF pilots killed and 4,000 troops taken prisoner. However, the Germans continued to believe that the inevitable invasion would be north of Dieppe, nearer Calais – an error that helped to make D-Day a success.

## LITERARY LINKS

It was in the Café Suisse in the Arcades de la Bourse that Oscar Wilde supposedly wrote *The Ballad of Reading Gaol*. Georges Simenon of Inspector Maigret fame mentions it in *L'Homme de Londres*, set in Dieppe. The 18th-century Café des Tribunaux, in place Puits Salé, is where Aubrey Beardsley, the illustrator, drank, and painter Walter Sickert is said to have told Gauguin to stick to banking.

Minister of Britain, even had a cross-Channel cable laid to maintain contact with London while on holiday.

### Cité de la Mer

Opened in 1992, this hi-tech attraction teaches landlubbers about the sea, from steering by stars and satellite navigation to the formation of cliffs and model boats. If you like you can follow the career of a fish, from sea to dinner plate.
*37 rue de l'Asile Thomas.*
*Tel: 02 35 06 93 20.*
*Open: daily. Admission charge.*

### Église de St-Jacques

There are cobwebs in the Jehan Ango oratory but this medieval church is being slowly restored. A memorial to the Canadians who died in the 1942 Dieppe raid is in a side chapel.
*Rue St Jacques. Open: daily.*
*Free admission.*

### Musée du Château

This well-preserved castle has local views by Impressionists Walter Sickert and Camille Pissarro, plus lithographs by Cubist Georges Braque, who

retired to nearby Varengeville. Take a look at the hand-carved ivory, especially the 18th-century figures, the *Four Seasons.*
*Rue Chastes. Tel: 02 35 06 61 99.*
*Open: daily, standard hours (see pp186–7). Closed: Sept–May, Tue.*
*Admission charge.*

St Jacques on the façade of the church in Dieppe dedicated to him

A stunning sunset at Étretat

## Étretat

The 19th-century author Alphonse Karr wrote: 'If I had to show a friend the sea for the first time, I would do so at Étretat.' Guy de Maupassant compared the Falaise d'Aval to 'a carved elephant dipping its trunk into the sea' while Maurice Leblanc used the 70-m (230-ft) high chalk needle as a hiding place for the stolen *Mona Lisa* in one of his *Arsène Lupin* books.

The towering cliffs, pierced by wind and waves to create *portes* (doorways), have fascinated man for thousands of years. The Romans built a road here from Lillebonne; Marie-Antoinette insisted on eating oysters specially raised here; and in the 19th century, the world and his wife came here by train for the casino and the theatre. The brave even went sea-bathing. Today, Étretat is no longer exotic. Camera tripods have replaced the easels of 19th-century artists Boudin, Corot and Manet, while the fishing community they painted is all but extinct. A few *caloges* (thatched cottages) have been rebuilt on the front as a reminder of yesteryear, but even the handsome, beamed covered market dates only from 1926, having been moved here from Lower Normandy. Nevertheless, the cliffs remain truly awesome: the Falaise d'Amont (upstream) to the north, the Falaise d'Aval (downstream) to the south (*see pp46–7*).

### Maison Maurice Leblanc

The Arsène Lupin connection is celebrated at Maurice Leblanc's former house. Visitors are guided on a clever interactive tour in the form of a game, which reveals the world of Leblanc's gentleman thief.
*Le Clos Arsène Lupin. Tel: 02 35 10 59 53. Open: Apr–Sept, daily, standard hours (see pp186–7); Oct–Mar, Fri, Sat & Sun. Closed: mid-Nov–mid-Dec. Admission charge.*

### Château des Aygues

This is a 19th-century seaside palace for European aristocracy who came to spend 'the season' at Étretat. It houses a fine collection of Chinese porcelain.
*Rue Offenbach. Tel: 02 35 28 92 77. Open: daily. Closed: Tue, except July–Sept. Admission charge.*

*Étretat is 28km (17 miles) north of Le Havre, via the D940.*

### Fécamp

Does the town's name derive from the Old Norse word *fisk* (fish), referring to the successful fishermen who dared to cross even the Atlantic for their catches? Or from *Ficicampum*, the place of the fig-tree? Supposedly, in the 1st century, a hollowed-out fig tree was washed ashore, carrying drops of Précieux Sang, the Holy Blood of Christ, in a lead casket. Certainly, Fécamp was a greater medieval pilgrimage site than even Mont-St-Michel.

### Abbatiale de la Trinité

Behind the altar in this lovely abbey church a white marble tabernacle holds the Précieux Sang; to the right is a footprint marking the appearance of an angel to bishops in AD 943.
*Rue des Forts. Tel: 02 35 28 84 39.*
*Open: daily. Admission charge.*

### Musée Centre des Arts

This interesting, eclectic collection includes an assortment of babies' feeding bottles amassed by one Docteur Dufour, a crusader against infant mortality.
*21 rue Alexandre-Legros. Tel: 02 35 28 31 99. Open: daily, standard hours (see pp186–7). Closed: Tue & Sept–June. Admission charge.*

### Museé des Terres-Neuvas et de la Pêche

This beachfront museum opened in 1988 to honour the long-haul cod fishermen, *morutiers*, who once spent months on end in frigid North Atlantic waters. The museum has displays on fishing and boat-building, nets and rescue services.
*27 boulevard Albert 1er. Tel: 02 35 28 31 99. Open: daily (see pp186–7). Closed: Tue except in July and Aug, when it's open daily. Admission charge.*

*A ticket for any of the three museums gives a discount for the other two.*

### Palais Bénédictine

From the outside, the Palais Bénédictine looks like a red-brick Disney fairy castle, but inside, the serious business of making the world-famous liqueur in the huge copper stills continues.

At the end of the tour you can look forward to a free tasting. There is also an art gallery and a museum here.
*110 rue Alexandre-le-Grand. Tel: 02 35 10 26 10; www.benedictine.fr*
*Open: daily. Closed: Jan. Admission charge.*

*Fécamp is 40km (25 miles) north of Le Havre, via the D925.*

---

**Bénédictine**
While visiting the Benedictine monastery in Fécamp, a Venetian monk named Don Bernardo Vincelli wrote down his recipe for an elixir to cure the sick; that was in 1510. In 1863, Alexandre le Grand, a local wine-merchant, found the instructions in an ancient tome and reinvented the greenish-yellow liqueur. Lemon peel, juniper oil, myrrh and saffron are among the 27 ingredients that, after a lengthy two-year process, result in Bénédictine. What was a cold cure is now a world-famous *digestif* (after-dinner drink).

A lingering reminder of an old taste of Normandy

# Walk: the cliffs of Étretat

These walks are not recommended for those with a fear of heights or with small children. The paths have been etched into the chalk over centuries and have few or no safety railings, while at the top the cliff edge is crumbling away. That said, these are two invigorating walks: one south, the other north of the town. Sensible shoes are recommended. *Allow half an hour for each walk.*

### Walk 1 – south to the Falaise d'Aval

#### 1 Place Victor Hugo
Start outside the Casino where the

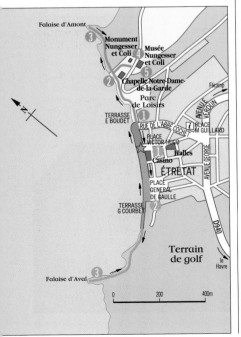

concrete promenade has been built to protect the town from the violent winter storms.
*Turn left along the promenade.*

#### 2 Terrasse G Courbet
Glass windbreaks on all four sides protect the outdoor cafés from breezy weather. Even in winter, surfboarders cavort in the cold, grey waves. A Noah's Ark houses the local sailing club and every morning oilskinned fishermen sell *carrelet* (plaice), *cabillaud* (cod) and *barbue* (brill) caught only minutes before. Beware: some visitors head south along the beach towards the *porte* (gateway), heedless of the large signs warning that tides can leave you stranded.
*Continue along the promenade. Climb the steps up the cliff.*

#### 3 Falaise d'Aval
After 93 concrete steps, a flint-filled path, worn into the hillside, leads to the top (*see p44*). Across the ravine to the left is a golf course. Bear right and, after 15 minutes, cross a narrow bridge to reach a small, rather grubby concrete

blockhouse. Paths, like white fingers, spray off to vantage points on the cliff edge. Now look back at the spectacular view across the bay that has attracted visitors for decades. *Return, but remember loose flints can make the downhill walk tricky under foot. Follow the promenade to the place Victor-Hugo.*

The sculpted heads of airmen Coli and Nungesser on the memorial at Étretat

### 3 Falaise d'Amont

If the Falaise d'Aval is terrifying, the Falaise d'Amont is humbling. A narrow cliff path cuts down to the sea, getting ever narrower. Sadly, visitors cannot resist carving their names in the chalk, which is layered with flints. At least there is a wooden handrail here with a ladder for the final descent to the beach, where the water churns remorselessly at the base of awesome cliffs.
*Return to the cliff top and the chapel.*

### 4 Monument Nungesser et Coli

Inland from the sailors' chapel is a car park and a needle-like memorial that is part bird, part Concorde, marking the efforts in 1927 of Nungesser and Coli, two aviators who died trying to fly the Atlantic.

### 5 Musée Nungesser et Coli

This museum is a tribute to the two aviators.
*Return to the promenade via the stairs.*

## Walk 2 – north to the Falaise d'Amont

### 1 Terrasse E Boudet
*From the place Victor-Hugo, pass the boules court.*
Out to sea, stumps of collapsed cliffs protrude from the water.
*At the end of the promenade, climb 83 steps on the new concrete path, past a park.*

### 2 Chapelle Notre-Dame de la Garde
At the top is a little-used granite chapel, a 1950 replacement for the original, destroyed in World War II. The gargoyles are fun: each is a metre-long seal. Now look back to the south for another sweeping panorama across the bay, to the arch in the Falaise d'Aval, so often painted at sunset.
*Follow signs to the Falaise d'Amont, a 10-minute walk.*

**Musée Nungesser et Coli**
*Tel: 02 35 27 07 47. Open: June–Sept, daily, and weekends in the spring. Admission charge.*

## Giverny

This quiet riverside village has become a shrine to Claude Monet, who lived here from 1883 until 1926. The two-storey pink house retains his personal furniture, mementoes, and fine collection of Japanese prints, but is spoiled by reproductions of his own works crammed on to some walls. Outside, the garden is still planted to the painter's design, while an underpass leads to the Oriental water garden with its bamboo, weeping willows and water lily ponds, which he also planned. Trying to savour the scene of the *Nymphéas* (water lily) series can be disappointing when reality is a group of camera-toting tourists standing on the curved Japanese bridge. Arrive out of season, however, and the magic can still work.

*Maison et Jardins de Claude Monet. Tel: 02 32 51 28 21; www.fondation-monet.com. Open: Apr–Oct, daily, except Mon. Admission charge.*

### Museé d'Art Américain

Opened in 1992, this low-profile museum examines the transatlantic connection inspired by Monet. He is shown in *The Wedding March*, painted by Theodore Robinson in 1892, following his stepdaughter and new American son-in-law, the painter Theodore Butler, down the (still recognisable) village street. There are several fine Impressionist-style works.

*99 rue Claude Monet. Tel: 02 32 51 94 65. Open: Apr–Oct, daily, except Mon. Admission charge.*

*Giverny is 76km (47 miles) west of Paris, in the Seine valley, off the D5.*

### Le Havre

Le Havre (meaning 'harbour') was built in 1517 to replace neighbouring Harfleur, which had silted up. In 1944, eight days of intensive bombing flattened the city; clearing the rubble took two years. The Herculean task of post-war reconstruction was relished by Auguste Perret.

Perret's High Modernist vision is reviled by many, but it is undoubtedly a masterwork of its genre. On the place de l'Hôtel de Ville, the town hall and its 72-m (236-ft) tall tower are dwarfed only by the

## CLAUDE MONET 1840–1926

Born in Paris, Monet grew up in Le Havre where he met Eugène Boudin and was inspired to capture the atmosphere of the seaside.

In the 1860s, Normandy was the cradle of Impressionism with Monet and friends meeting at the Ferme St Siméon in Honfleur, in Trouville, and along the River Seine. They were all impressed and inspired by the multi-hued shimmering, ever-changing light, but it was Monet's *Impression, Sunrise* that gave the movement a name in 1874. Recurring themes are his gardens at Giverny and the west front of Rouen Cathedral.

In his later years, when he was suffering from cataracts, his failing eyesight led to bigger and even bolder canvases such as the *Nymphéas* (water lilies) series. However, his renowned 'impressionistic' style was developed decades before.

109m (358 ft) of the St Joseph Church bell tower. In 2005, the restored city was named a UNESCO World Heritage Site. Le Havre is one of Europe's largest ports. The attractive Ste-Adresse district, to the west, is the posh part of town where Monet grew up.

## Cathédrale Notre-Dame

Somehow this building managed to survive the bombing. Its eccentric mix of architectural styles puts Gothic and Renaissance cheek-to-cheek: a square, grey 16th-century bell tower next to the warm, pink 17th-century portal.
*Rue Ed Lang. Open: daily. Free admission.*

## Église St-Joseph

Minimalist on the outside, this Perret-designed concrete church comes to life inside, thanks to the brilliance of the stained-glass windows.
*Boulevard François 1er. Open: daily. Free admission.*

## Musée de l'Ancien Havre

In a splendid 17th-century house in the oldest part of Le Havre, the history of the city is told. Apart from the architectural theme, one room is devoted to local folk music.
*1 rue Jérôme Bellarmato. Tel: 02 35 42 27 90. Open: Wed–Sun, standard hours (see pp186–7).*
*Admission charge.*

## Musée des Beaux-Arts André Malraux

This striking building offers a view of the sea through a concrete sculpture nicknamed the 'eye'. Inside are 200 paintings by the 'Roi des ciels' (King of the Skies) Eugène Boudin, who encouraged the early Impressionists. Raoul Dufy, a Le Havre native, is also well represented.
*Boulevard Clémenceau.*
*Tel: 02 35 19 62 62. Open: Wed–Mon, standard hours (see pp186–7).*
*Admission charge.*

Nasturtiums below the pergola in Monet's gardens at Giverny

### Abbaye de Jumièges

Tucked among fields on a bend of the River Seine, this Benedictine abbey was a centre of wealth and learning for 700 years (*see p37*) until, after the Revolution of 1789, it was blown up and treated as a ready-made quarry. The ruins, now with the 27-m (89-ft) high nave open to the sky, are hauntingly beautiful. The west front, with its massive twin towers, is a classic example of Norman building.

*27km (17 miles) west of Rouen, on the north bank of the Seine, on the D143. Tel: 02 35 37 24 02. Open: daily. Admission charge.*

### Lyons-la-Forêt

Scenically located in the heart of the vast beech forest, this photogenic cluster of brick, flint and half-timbered houses centres on the place Benserade (named after the 17th-century poet born in Paris).

Antiques shops and *bistrots* look on to the medieval covered market, supported by 27 wooden pillars. At the bottom of the rue de la République on the right, a plaque states that Maurice Ravel composed *Le Tombeau de Couperin*

(1917) and orchestrated Mussorgsky's *Pictures at an Exhibition* (1922) while living here at Le Fresne, a mock Norman house.

### Château Fleury la Forêt

At the end of a parade of lime trees, this 17th-century pink-brick château has a good collection of dolls.

*7km (4 miles) northeast of Lyons-la-Forêt. Tel: 02 32 49 63 91; www.chateau-fleury-la-foret.com. Open: mid-June–mid-Sept, daily, afternoons; mid-Sept–Nov & Mar–mid-June, Sat, Sun & bank holidays. Closed: Dec, Jan, Feb. Admission charge.*

### Château de Vascoeuil

More an arts centre than a château, this fortified house exhibits contemporary sculpture in the gardens and art in the beautifully restored *colombier* (dovecote). A small cottage contains memorabilia of the 19th-century historian Jules Michelet who lived here.

*11km (7 miles) northwest of Lyons-la-Forêt. Tel: 02 35 23 62 35. Open: July–Aug, daily, 11am–6.30pm; afternoons only, rest of year. Closed: mid-Nov–mid-Mar. Admission charge.*

The beautiful ruins of the Abbey de Jumièges

### GUY DE MAUPASSANT (1850–93)

This great writer was born in Fécamp but spent his early years in the Château de Miromesnil, near Dieppe. He studied in Rouen and Yvetot, where he rejected religion. His relationships with women were unsuccessful and he became a pessimist. Maupassant's writing was nurtured by Gustave Flaubert and Émile Zola and his short story *Boule de Suif* was an overnight success in 1880. In all, he produced 300 short stories and six novels, most set in or about Normandy where he spent much of his time at Étretat. He died, aged 43, of syphilis.

*Lyons-la-Forêt is 35km (22 miles) east of Rouen, in the heart of the forest, off the N31.*

## Château de Miromesnil

Save this for a fine day, to enjoy the park, formal gardens and restored kitchen garden. The plain-looking chapel among beech trees reveals an ornate interior with painted statues and carved wood. Inside the 16th-century château are mementoes of Guy de Maupassant (*see box*) and statesmen such as Hue de Miromesnil, an 18th-century Chancellor of France.
*Tourville-sur-Arques, 6km (3¹/₂ miles) south of Dieppe, off the N27. Tel: 02 35 85 02 80; www.chateaumiromesnil.com. Open: Apr–Oct, daily, afternoons; gardens open for self-guided visits with extended hours in July and Aug. Admission charge.*

## Pont-Audemer

The River Risle divides to surround the old part of this thriving town, long-famous for leather. Its nickname 'Normandy's Little Venice' may be an exaggeration, but the fine 17th-century, half-timbered houses along canals crossed by wooden footbridges are distinctly romantic. Modern stained-glass windows complement 16th-century glass in the 11th-century Church of St-Ouen, which remains unfinished after 500 years.
*Just off the A13 motorway, 50km (31 miles) west of Rouen.*

## Château de Robert-le-Diable

Debatable legend alleges that Robert the Magnificent, father of William the Conqueror, built the castle that now lies in artful semi-ruin alongside the motorway. Somewhat touristy but amusing for children, the château exhibits a 20-m (66-ft) *drakkar* (longship), along with wax models telling the Viking story and the life of William the Conqueror. His father would hardly recognise the fortress he built, with the motorway above and the industrial port of Rouen below.
*Near Moulineaux, just off the A13 motorway, 15km (9 miles) southwest of Rouen.*
*Tel: 02 35 18 02 36. Open: Mar–Nov, daily. Admission charge.*

Half-timbered houses tumbling down the hill at Lyons-la-Forêt

## Ry

Called Yonville l'Abbaye in Gustave Flaubert's novel *Madame Bovary*, this undistinguished village has cashed in on its literary connection. Emma Bovary was based on Delphine Couturier, the doctor's wife, who died in what is now the chemist's shop. The pharmacy in the novel is now the dry cleaners . . . and Ry's old chemist's is now in the **Musée d'Automates**, many of whose 500 moving mechanical figures recreate scenes from the book.

*20km (12 miles) northeast of Rouen, on the D13. Galerie Bovary, Musée d'Automates, place Flaubert. Tel: 02 35 23 61 44. Open: Easter–Oct, Sat–Mon, afternoons; July & Aug, daily, afternoons. Admission charge.*

## St Martin-de-Boscherville

Unlike the nearby ruined abbeys of St-Wandrille and Jumièges, the Caumont stone of St-Martin-de-Boscherville shines a brilliant white, thanks to recent renovation. Built originally for the Augustinians, the abbey was taken over by the Benedictines in 1114. They were ejected during the French Revolution

Flower shop in Ry, a village made famous by its connections with Flaubert's *Madame Bovary*

and this impressive building is now the parish church. The monastery garden is being restored, while archaeologists have found traces of a pagan temple dating from 100 BC under the 12th-century chapterhouse.

*10km (6 miles) west of Rouen, off the D982. Tel: 02 35 32 10 82. Open: Apr–Oct, daily; Nov–Mar, afternoons. Admission charge.*

## St Wandrille

To get the best out of a visit to this abbey, take a tour with a Benedictine monk (*see p37*). Since St Wandrille settled here around 650, communities have come and gone. After the Revolution, 100 years passed before the monks returned; the present community has lasted since 1931. At first glance this looks like a château, but inside are the skeletal ruins of the 13th-century abbey church and the early 16th-century flamboyant Gothic cloisters. The monks worship in their 'new' church, a 13th-century Norman tithe barn they took down and reassembled in 1967. Listening to Gregorian chants ringing out, even non-believers are moved.

*30km (19 miles) west of Rouen, off the D982. Tel: 02 35 96 23 11; www.st-wandrille.com. Open: daily. Guided tours available. Telephone for times. Admission charge.*

## Valmont

Only the Lady Chapel stands intact among the ruins, but the delicate arches and altarpiece of the Renaissance interior retain their elegance. This Benedictine abbey was founded by the Estouteville family, made famous by Victor Hugo in

Although much of the Abbey of St Wandrille is in ruins, there is still much to see and enjoy

*The Hunchback of Notre-Dame*; their ancestral home across the river features a 900-year-old keep.
*10km (6 miles) east of Fécamp on the D17. Abbaye tel: 02 35 27 34 92. Guided tours only: Apr–Sept, Wed–Mon. Admission restricted when restoration is in progress.*

## Vernon

Photographers love the half-timbered house perched on the remaining stone arches of the medieval bridge across the River Seine. Vernon marks the ancient border with France but is now known for making the Ariane space rocket. More half-timbered houses surround the 12th-century church, whose striking modern glass dates from 1993.

### Château Bizy

Two kilometres (1 mile) west of Vernon, this Italianate mansion has a large park, fine furniture inside, and a vintage car collection in the palatial stables.
*Tel: 02 32 51 00 82. Open: Apr–Oct, Tue–Sun; Mar, Sat & Sun, afternoons. Admission charge.*
*Vernon is 80km (50 miles) northwest of Paris, on the N15.*

## Villequier

Every French student reads Victor Hugo's poem *A Villequier*, mourning the death of his daughter, Léopoldine, and her husband, Charles Vacquerie, who were drowned here in 1843 by the River Seine's notorious tidal bore (*see p37*). In the picnic area at the eastern edge of the village stands a statue of Hugo: left hand raised to his cheek, he stares at the spot. Two lines from the poem are carved on the monument:
*Il faut que l'herbe pousse et que*
*    les enfants meurent;*
*Je le sais, ô mon Dieu!*
Grass must grow,
    and children must die;
I realise that, O Lord!

### Maison Vacquerie, Musée Victor Hugo

Fans come for photos, rare books and drawings of the great man (1802–85). The house has been extensively refurbished.
*Rue Ernest-Binet. Tel: 02 35 56 78 31. Open: daily, standard hours (see pp186–7). Admission charge.*

*Villequier is 47km (29 miles) east of Le Havre, on the D81.*

Now a museum, the elegant villa at Villequier was Victor Hugo's home

# Central Normandy

Centring on Calvados, the *département* that gave its name to a famous drink, this is the Normandy everyone recognises: dairy-rich meadows and renowned cheeses, the glamour of Deauville and the romance of Honfleur, cradle of Impressionist art. It is also William the Conqueror country: born in Falaise, buried in Caen.

The Conqueror's castle at Caen

This area is renowned for its famous cheeses, named after the places they come from – Camembert, Livarot and Pont-l'Évêque. Nowadays, although most of these are factory-made, you can still visit several farms where *lait cru* (unpasteurised milk) produces the full flavour that one French gourmet evocatively described as 'kissing the feet of God'.

## Central Normandy

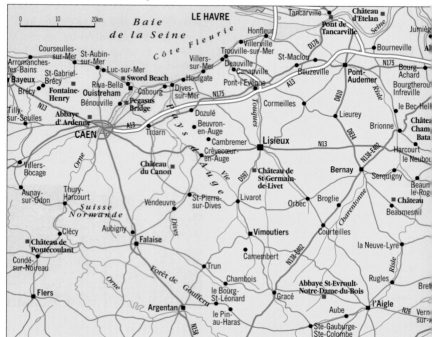

Deauville is like a theatre without a play for much of the year, until the summer when the rich and famous, paparazzi and budding starlets turn the *planches* (promenade) into a cabaret – no wonder the down-to-earth prefer Trouville next door. Cabourg is snooty and sophisticated, remembering its past just as Marcel Proust did, in his writing about his childhood holidays here. The western resorts would be unremarkable were it not for Jour J (D-Day), a turning point in world history (*see pp66–9*) recorded in a string of small museums.

If Honfleur wins the 'prettiest harbour' prize, then Beuvron-en-Auge merits 'prettiest village' over other rivals in the Pays d'Auge region. Expect crowds at weekends and in summer. The châteaux of Crèvecoeur-en-Auge and St-Germain-de-Livet are straight out of fairy tales.

Le Bec-Hellouin was once the intellectual and spiritual heart of Normandy, thanks to the clever monks at its abbey. Lisieux is one of the world's great pilgrimage centres: Ste Thérèse, whose photograph appears all over Normandy, came to live here in 1877.

Brionne, with its ruined keep, and Flers in the Orne valley are just two places that produce a 'this is the real France' reaction from visitors. Don't expect to ski in the Suisse Normande, the hills and valleys south of Caen; but you can go canoeing and hang-gliding, mountain biking and hiking.

With a castle, two abbeys and an exquisite church, Caen has one foot planted firmly in the past, but the lively university and the replacement of old industry with high technology keeps the other foot in the future. Between them is Le Mémorial – the museum for peace.

Windows in heady Calvados

# Caen

'. . . the most prepossessing . . . and most happily situated of towns. Its streets are the handsomest, its churches, public buildings and walks the finest of their kind; and from this town have come the brightest wits and intelligences of their country.' So wrote diarist Madame de Sévigné in 1689, and though such praise may smack of public-relations hype, the capital of the Calvados *département* is today a balance of glorious monuments and post-World War II construction. But Caen is a city that prefers to look forward, investing heavily in the technology of tomorrow. Between Caen and Hérouville-St-Clair, northwest of the city, is Synergia, a hi-tech industrial park. GANIL, the Grand Accelerateur National d'Ions Lourds, is an international research project into how matter is made, using a heavy ion accelerator.

Caen's population of 150,000 includes 22,000 students at the university, which is best known for its faculties of science and French literature. The students add to the liveliness of the city, especially on a Thursday night in the pubs and cafés around the campus. Students also come from all over Europe to attend the Centre Chorégraphique National, to train as dancers.

The capital of Basse Normandie, Caen was the favourite town of William the Conqueror, whose massive castle is the focal point, positioned halfway between the great abbeys built by him and his wife as penance for breaking the rule forbidding cousins to marry. After he became King of England, rebellion led to battles. The English were expelled in 1204, only to return in 1346 when King Edward III's troops filled a hundred boats with booty from the looted city. After the French defeat at Agincourt in 1415, it took 33 years to get rid of the English 'Goddons', presumably named for the soldiers' expletives.

## CAEN STONE

The creamy whiteness of Caen limestone gives it the appearance of being too soft for building material, yet it has created magnificent monuments not just in France but also in England. Caen stone was floated down the River Orne and across the English Channel for use in the cathedrals of Canterbury and Winchester as well as Westminster Abbey.

When King Henry V reoccupied Normandy in 1415, he commandeered the quarries solely for building his royal palaces. In World War II, caves dug into the sides of these limestone pits south of the city sheltered locals from bombing.

Caen's links to the sea are the River Orne and the 12-km (7¹/₂-mile) long canal to Ouistreham, developed by Brittany Ferries as a ferry port. You can join locals at the lively Friday farmers' market in the place St-Sauveur and the rue St-Pierre, walk in the old town (*see pp64–5*), or visit Le Mémorial, the hi-tech museum of peace with its park, created for the 50th anniversary of D-Day in 1994. This is located on the northwest side of the city.

Nos 52 and 54 rue St-Pierre, superb early 16th-century timbering and detail

## Caen

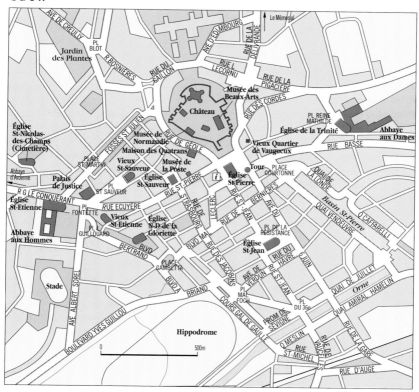

## Abbaye aux Dames

The façade of the abbey church, l'Église de la Trinité, looks a little strange, thanks to some fanciful restoration in the mid-19th century. Its towers were reduced to their stunted state during the Hundred Years' War. Next door, the convent buildings now house the Regional Council's offices. Well-informed guides explain the varied history of the abbey structure, which spans every historical epoch. Inside the Abbey church, recent cleaning has brought back the buttery tones of native stone. The simple, sombre lines and planes are classic Norman style, with geometric, animal and grotesque motifs adding texture and whimsy. Visit the church in the morning, if possible. On sunny days, a blood-red light streams through the stained glass, dramatically illuminating a simple black marble slab on the chancel floor, the tomb of Queen Mathilda.

*Rue des Chanoines. Tel: 02 31 06 98 98. Guided tours of the Abbey and Church daily 2.30pm & 4pm. Church open daily 8am–7pm, closed midday. Free admission.*

## Abbaye aux Hommes

William was finally laid to rest in the Church of St-Etienne, twice as long and twice as wide as la Trinité. Today, houses crowd up against its walls and the stark west front is almost lost in the small square off rue Guillaume-le-Conquérant. The Hôtel de Ville (Town Hall), formerly the 18th-century monastery, abuts the south side and only from its gardens can the scale of this church be appreciated. It was built in 11 years, with money appropriated from a conquered England; seven spires

Glowing Caen stone on the convent buildings of the Abbaye aux Dames

Interior of the monastery of Abbaye aux Hommes, now part of Caen town hall

mark the spot where construction began in 1066. The high interior gives a tremendous feeling of space and repairs over the centuries have been in keeping with its austerity. When the wooden roof of the nave was rebuilt in stone in 1130, the Gothic vaulting was kept simple, and when the lantern tower collapsed in 1566, the prior, Dom Jean de Baillehache, copied the original. In World War II the church suffered little in the long battle for Caen; thankfully, the Resistance had managed to alert the Allies that hundreds were sheltering inside.

*Rue Guillaume-le-Conquérant.*
*Tel: 02 31 30 42 81. Open: daily. Guided tours: 9.30am, 11am, 2.30pm & 4pm. English-language tours available in July & Aug. Admission charge.*

### Le Château

The remains of William's 11th-century castle are impressive. Within the massive walls and towers are public gardens and museums: the 900-year-old Echiquier (Exchequer), now beautifully restored, holds temporary exhibitions, as does the tiny Chapelle St-Georges. Picture this back in 1418, crowded with a dozen knights ready to receive the Order of the Bath from King Henry V of England. Visitors can watch archaeological excavations and restoration work to the rear of the ramparts.

### Musée des Beaux-Arts

After a major face-lift, the museum's highly rated collection of 16th- and 17th-century art is now properly lit and chronologically arranged. Classic 19th-century seaside scenes such as Courbet's *La Mer à Langrune* and Boudin's *La Plage de Tourgéville* can be seen along with works by Monet, Vuillard, Bonnard and Dufy.

*Tel: 02 31 85 28 63. Open: daily, standard hours (see pp186–7). Admission charge.*

### Musée de Normandie

This fascinating 'then' and 'now' explanation of Norman life is housed in the Château. Maps prove that Roman roads are still main routes; models contrast the 'open' farmyards of the Cotentin Peninsula with the 'closed' design around Argentan. Half-timbering with stone, brick and wood is demonstrated, and there are cider presses and copper stills for making calvados. Admire the stunning wedding dress of '*blonde*' (ivory silk) lace, discover what a *tyrosemiophile* is, but don't miss the grave of a blacksmith surrounded by his tools.

*Tel: 02 31 30 47 60. Open: June–Sept, daily, 9.30am–6pm; Oct–May, Wed–Mon, 9.30am–6pm. Admission charge for exhibitions.*

### Le Mémorial

A jagged split in the smooth white façade is just one symbol of the 20th century's *faillité de la paix*, the failure of peace. This ultramodern memorial-cum-museum has aroused much controversy. Does it over-dramatise war? By selling models of warplanes and T-shirts with doves, does it become 'just another tourist attraction'? Decide for yourself.

Inside, a Hawker Typhoon aircraft hangs over a pile of rubble from Caen, 'the martyred city'. A spiralling ramp leads down into chaos: Fascism and Communism rise; Wall Street crashes; screens blaze with the torches of Nuremberg rallies. Next, darkened rooms emphasise the Depression and progression into war. The plight of the Jews is movingly portrayed with individual stories personalising the horrifying statistics. Most significant for the French, however, is the question: '40 million collaborators – 40 million resisters?' The self-examination accuses the French militia of being the 'zealous arm of the occupying power'.

The seven-spired church of St Etienne

Then, suddenly, you are in a conventional museum of World War II, with guns and uniforms, maps and models, plus relics and films of the Battle of Normandy. The research centre focuses on the war and there is a gallery dedicated to Nobel Peace Prize winners. *Esplanade Eisenhower. Tel: 02 31 06 06 45; www.memorial-caen.fr. Open: Feb–Sept, daily, 9am–7pm; Oct–Dec, daily, 9.30am–6pm. Closed: Dec 25 & Jan. Admission charge.*

## Musée de la Poste et des Techniques de Communication

A long name for a small museum of postage stamps and communications, from the telegraph to the telephone, housed in the finest remaining half-timbered structures in Caen.
*52 rue St-Pierre. Tel: 02 31 50 12 20. Open: mid-June–mid-Sept, Tue–Sat, standard hours (see p186); mid-Sept–mid-June, afternoons only. Admission charge.*

## Église St-Pierre

Traffic rumbles round this church. Inside, the flamboyant Renaissance stone carving is remarkable, particularly the capitals of the second and third pillars on the north side of the nave, where Sir Lancelot and Sir Gawain, knights of the round table, can be seen in the company of munching rabbits in a field of cabbages.
*Rue Montoir-Poissonerie.*

## Vieux Quartier de Vaugueux

All of Caen once looked like this cluster of tiny, cobbled streets east of the castle. The ancient houses are now a United Nations of restaurants.

Complex vaulting in one of the side chapels of Église St-Pierre

'Stark he was . . . so harsh and cruel . . . that none withstood his will; all men were obliged to be obedient, and to follow his will, if they would have lands or even life.' So the *Anglo-Saxon Chronicle* described William the Bastard, born in 1027 of a romantic alliance that is legendary (*see p78*). He became Duke of Normandy at the age of seven and by 20 was a battle-hardened leader. At Domfront, he challenged Geoffrey Martel, Count of Anjou, to personal combat; the Count backed down. When the citizens of Alençon mocked him, jeering 'Tanner' from the walls, he cut off the hands and feet of 32 offenders after capturing the city.

William invaded England after the death of King Edward the Confessor. As the king's cousin, his claim to the throne preceded that of Harold, who was only Edward's brother-in-law. Several years before, William had tricked Harold into swearing on holy relics to respect the Duke's right to the English throne.

Short, muscular and with a vile temper, William was also far-sighted and just, a harsh but efficient administrator who gave his barons land in exchange for their loyalty, cleverly spreading these assets across the country to prevent any ideas of 'empire-building'.

William was happily married for 30 years to his cousin, Mathilda of Flanders. Injured in a 'skirmish' with the French king, the Conqueror died in Rouen in 1087, at the age of 60, the most famous Norman of all.

With its abbeys and castle, Caen has one foot firmly planted in the past

# Walk: Caen

Caen was at the centre of the D-Day attack in 1944 and was devastated by bombing and artillery fire. Miraculously, some of the medieval town survived and can be seen on this short stroll (*see pp56–62* for more details of places to see).

*Allow about 45 minutes.*

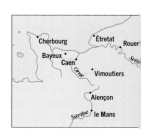

*Start at the Église St-Pierre, near the tourist office.*

### 1  Église St-Pierre

Although Caen's two 11th-century abbeys are more famous, this is the parish church of the city and, as such, has attracted generous gifts over the centuries. The soaring 78-m (256-ft) spire built in 1317 was destroyed in 1944 but has been rebuilt.

*Enter rue St-Pierre.*

### 2  Rue St-Pierre

This pedestrianised street used to have several sections, such as the *confiserie* (confectioner's) and the *mercerie* (haberdashery), named for the products

sold there. Mostly post-war, it still has several medieval buildings housing high-quality shops selling chocolates, jewellery and cakes. Just after the Pavillon Christofle, peer through a gate on the left: the entry looks centuries old. Across on the right, No 54 is the Musée de la Poste (Postal Museum) in one of the finest 16th-century half-timbered houses in Caen, complete with carvings of saints.

*Cross rue de Strasbourg and turn right.*

### 3  Rue Froide

The Église St-Sauveur used to be called Notre-Dame-de-Froide-Rue and is, unusually, built on a north-south axis. A plan on the left-hand wall of rue

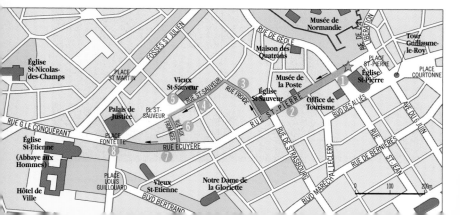

Froide shows the area in 1817. Little passages to the left and right, such as rue de la Monnaie, are atmospheric. No 22 bis, with its grimy archway, timbered ceiling and old courtyard, has not changed in centuries. Diners at l'Amandier restaurant enjoy medieval surroundings.

*At the end of rue Froide, turn left on to rue St-Sauveur.*

### 4  Rue St-Sauveur

Rooms on the upper levels of these houses still have ancient beams that are visible through the windows. Across the street looms the bulk of another St-Sauveur, Vieux St-Sauveur. Only its 12th-century tower survived the war. Restoration continues at this old butter-market church.

### 5  Place St-Sauveur

Apart from being a useful car park, this square has handsome 18th-century mansions overlooking a rather pompous statue of Louis XIV dressed as a Roman emperor. Until the last century a pillory still stood here, where the open-air market is held on Fridays.

Oak carving on the 16th-century Musée de la Poste, rue St-Pierre

Typical yellow-grey stone houses in the attractive town of Caen

*Leave the square via the rue aux Fromages.*

### 6  Rue aux Fromages

After a few steps, the atmosphere becomes medieval thanks to cobbles and half-timbered buildings housing, appropriately, antique dealers.

*Turn right into rue Ecuyère.*

### 7  Rue Ecuyère

More antique dealers line this wide, pedestrianised street, an extension of rue St-Pierre. On the right, No 32 has a barred peephole; on the left, No 42, the Hôtel des Ecuyers, dates from the 15th century and was later the home of a Vicomte de Caen.

*Continue to place Fontette.*

### 8  Place Fontette

On the right is the Palais de Justice, the handsome law courts, complete with Corinthian pillars. On the far side, the bridge offers an excellent view of the Abbaye aux Hommes and the Hôtel de Ville (town hall) which took over the 18th-century monastery buildings in 1965.

# Tour: the D-Day beaches

This 140-km (87-mile) route, from the mouth of the River Orne to the neck of the Cotentin Peninsula, follows the D-Day beaches past monuments and museums honouring the invasion forces.

*Allow at least half a day, more with stops.*

*Leave Caen on the D515 for Ouistreham. Turn off on the D141 to Bénouville and Pegasus Bridge.*

## 1 Pegasus Bridge

The eastern flank of the invasion is named for the emblem of the British 5th Parachute Brigade: this bridge and café were the first to be liberated in the early hours of 6 June, 1944. Too narrow for traffic, the old iron bridge was removed in 1993, but can be seen in the nearby museum (*see p81*).

*Return to the D515 for Ouistreham. Follow the Circuit du Débarquement signs.*

## 2 Ouistreham/Riva-Bella

A grim blockhouse, part of Germany's 'Atlantic Wall', survives one block inland. A small Commando museum across from the casino and a memorial in nearby dunes commemorate the first French troops to return to their native soil. A 12th-century church and *belle époque* villas add classic seaside appeal.

*Follow the D514 through resorts with streets named after D-Day heroes and tanks in main squares. Langrune is the border between Sword and Juno Beaches. In St-Aubin and Bernières, memorials to*

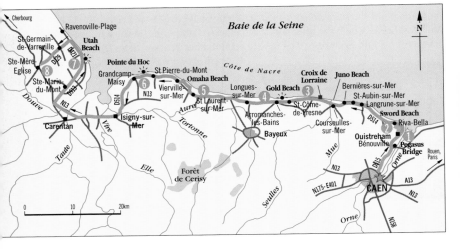

*the Canadian forces stand alongside neat white bathing huts.*

### 3 Courseulles-sur-Mer
Fishing boats bob beneath a gigantic cross of Lorraine, where General de Gaulle, leader of the Free French, triumphantly returned on 14 June. This is the end of Juno and the beginning of Gold Beach.
*Continue on the D514 past St-Côme-de-Fresne where, high on the cliffs, an orientation platform shows who came from where on D-Day.*

### 4 Arromanches-les-Bains
Remnants of a Mulberry harbour, floated from England, are still visible offshore; the museum tells the story *(see p69 & p96).*
*Follow the D514 to Longues, where the German battery remains, and through Port-en-Bessin, whose museum features shipwrecks hoisted from the deep. On the D514, follow the sign to Omaha Beach, turning right on to the single-track road.*

### 5 Omaha Beach
A wooden stile guards the rose-bordered path leading to a fortified point. The main concentration of American troops landed below.
*The lane leads to a vast American cemetery with rows of white crosses. Return to the D514, passing Vierville with its three-sided memorial to the US National Guard. At Criqueville-en-Bessin, turn right to Pointe du Hoc.*

### 6 Pointe du Hoc
Bleak and grim, the force of attack and defence is still felt here, thanks to

craters, semi-ruined bunkers and twisted steel wire. The US Rangers suffered horrific losses storming these crumbling brown cliffs.
*Return to the D514. Turn right towards Grandcamp-Maisy with its Ranger Museum. Join the N13 towards Cherbourg; exit on the D913 for Ste-Marie-du-Mont, where signs in the village recount local events on D-Day. Continue to Utah Beach.*

### 7 Utah Beach
A pink bollard marked '00' is the first kilometre-marker on la Voie de la Liberté, the road to European liberty.
*Take the D421 towards Ravenoville-Plage. Watch for the D129 on the left; turn on to Davis Rd, one of many named after non-commissioned soldiers who died here on D-Day. Take this to Ste-Mère-Église via St-Germain-de-Varreville.*

### 8 Ste-Mère-Église
The western flank of the D-Day landing was secured by US paratroops. Visit the excellent museum *(see p108).*

Sands of history at Omaha Beach

# D-Day

It takes only a matter of minutes to drive the 14km (9 miles) from Ouistreham to Caen; in 1944, it took Allied troops 34 days to fight their way from the beaches to the city. Moreover, the ferocity of the fighting after D-Day and the length of the Battle of Normandy are often forgotten in the blaze of military glory surrounding what was code-named 'Operation Overlord'.

The Allies worked hard to fool the Germans into believing that the invasion would attack the Pas de Calais across the narrow neck of the English Channel. Instead, it was directed at the 80-km (50-mile) wide stretch of Normandy coast between the Caen Canal in the east and the base of the Cotentin Peninsula in the west. In the early hours of 6 June, 135,000 troops and 20,000 vehicles landed on five sections, or beaches: Sword, Juno, Gold (British and Canadian forces), Omaha and Utah (US forces) between 6.30 and 7.30am.

Earlier, just after midnight, paratroopers dropped to secure the eastern and western flanks. The 4,000 ships, covered by 5,800 bombers and 4,900 fighters, constituted the greatest invasion force in history: the German Seventh Army, with its six Panzer divisions and 36 infantry divisions, was taken by surprise.

Nevertheless, the invasion was not easy; despite mine-removal tanks for the infantry there were 11,000 casualties including 2,500 dead on 6 June. The American 1st Division had a desperate struggle to capture Omaha Beach, overlooked by the massive defences on the elevated Pointe du Hoc.

Back-up support was vital; fresh troops, vehicles and ammunition ferried across in the invasion's wake used the unique, floating Mulberry Harbour, towed across the Channel to Arromanches. German reinforcements held up the advance and it was three weeks before Cherbourg and the Cotentin Peninsula were taken. The first 48 days' fighting cost 117,000 German casualties, the Allies a further 122,000, but Hitler's refusal to retreat played into the Allies' hands; the Germans were trapped in a pincer move in the Falaise Pocket and by 21 August the Battle of Normandy was over. Paris was liberated on 25 August, 1944.

Facing page above: one of the many memorials; below: Sherman tank at Courseulles, Juno Beach Above: Sword Beach today; left: Liberty Way marker

### Anet

Never underestimate the charm of an older woman. Henry II was just a 12-year-old prince when he fell under the spell of Diane de Poitiers, the beautiful 32-year-old widow of the powerful Lord of Anet. Although Henry married Catherine de' Medici, his mistress Diane effectively ran France for over a decade. The 'queen without a throne' lavished attention on Anet in the mid-1500s, transforming it into an Italianate palace with huge courtyards and formal gardens on the banks of the River Eure.

Architect Philibert Delorme, who designed the Tuileries, Fontainebleau and Chenonceau, rated Anet his finest work. The best tiles and tapestries, along with sculpture by masters such as Benvenuto Cellini, completed the magnificence. Unfortunately, much of the complex was pulled down in the early 19th century, but one wing and a chapel are open to the public. Note the gatehouse: above the clock stands a stag at bay, surrounded by four dogs which would have moved when the clock struck.

*Tel: 02 37 41 90 07. Open: Apr–Oct, daily (except Tue) afternoons; winter, Sat & Sun, afternoons. Admission charge.*

### Ivry-la-Bataille

Just across the river, the name recalls the victory of Henri IV over the Duke of Mayenne and the Catholic League in 1590. The king supposedly stayed at 5 rue de Garennes. The church of St-Martin, with its splendid tower, is another Diane de Poitiers/Philibert Delorme venture.

*Anet is on the River Eure, 16km (10 miles) north of Dreux on the D928.*

Lining up for paradise – the six noble lords of Aubigny

Beuvron-en-Auge is genuinely picturesque and correspondingly popular

## Aubigny

Just north of Falaise on the N158 is this small village, known for the six Lords of Aubigny. These life-sized statues kneel facing the altar in the chancel of the church, their (sculpted) clothes reflecting their times – from 1625 to 1786. Note the expectant smile on number five, unlike the devout expressions of the others.

## Château de Beaumesnil

This soft-pink brick and stone Baroque extravagance is a 17th-century mini-palace, complete with formal gardens and moat. Owned by the Furstenberg Foundation, it is known for its library of 17th- and 18th-century tomes and a museum recording the history of book-binding.
*13km (8 miles) southeast of Bernay. Tel: 02 32 44 40 09; www.chateaubeaumesnil.com. Open: Easter–June, Fri–Mon, afternoons; July–Aug, daily from 11am; Sept, Wed–Mon, afternoons. Admission charge.*

## Le Bec-Hellouin

The sleepy air of 'Le Bec' belies its role in history. In 1042, Lanfranc, an Italian intellectual, joined the monastic community, transformed it into a seat of learning and became Archbishop of Canterbury after the Conquest of England in 1066. Bec's importance also grew: the abbey church was one of the largest in Europe, but was pulled down after the Revolution, like so many others. The 15th-century Tour de St-Nicolas remains, however, and the view over the Risle Valley from the top is worth climbing the 201 steps. The 18th-century dormitories were used by the army until 1948 when the Benedictine monks revived the place's religious heritage.
*23km (14 miles) northeast of Bernay, on the D130. Tel: 02 32 43 72 60. Open: daily, standard hours (see pp186–7). Admission charge.*

## Bernay

A busy, small town that escaped wartime bombing, Bernay is worth a stop to admire the 11th-century abbey church and carved façades on medieval houses in streets such as rue Gaston Follope, with its antiques shops.
*57km (35 miles) southwest of Rouen, on the N138.*

## Beavron-en-Auge

This picture-postcard village in the Pays d'Auge, with half-timbered houses on the main square, a covered market and a chapel, is famous for its cheese, cider and horses. Parking is difficult in summer and on fine weekends.
*30km (19 miles) due east of Caen, on the D49, between the N13 and the N175.*

Although Norman castles, cathedrals and abbeys set new standards for monumental structures, the region also developed distinctive domestic architecture.

## Farmhouses

The sea-going ancestry of the Norsemen is reflected in their farmhouses. The shape resembles inverted *drakkars* (longships), oriented east-west to get the maximum sunshine. Long and narrow, these thatched houses always had the outside staircase at the sheltered east end; the west end, facing the prevailing wind, was shaped like the ship's prow. The irises planted along the roof ridge are more than mere decoration: the strong roots bind together the thatch and the clay inserted along the ridge acts as a seal.

## Dovecotes

*Colombiers* (dovecotes) were often the first target for destruction by mobs

during the French Revolution because the feudal system permitted local lords to keep pigeons which gobbled up grain from the peasants' fields. Yet the handsome, brick-built cylinders or octagons still dot the landscape. Many have been restored. Some are thatched, others tiled or covered in slate, and all have conical roofs. Since they provided fresh meat year-round, these were valuable assets. Some have chequer-board patterns of flint or glazed bricks; others have elaborately carved stone doorways, complete with coats of arms. All have a *larmier*, or ledge round the middle to stop rats and mice from climbing up and in. Inside were dozens of *boulins* (niches) for the pigeons and a rotating ladder for the keepers to collect eggs and birds.

## Manor houses

Normandy's manor houses are a delight, but, since most are privately owned, few visitors see more than the intriguing exteriors. The end of the Hundred Years' War with England (1450) sparked a boom in building. Though the advent of the cannon made castles redundant, protection was still needed, but from brigands not armies. So, these houses

have turreted towers, streams diverted into moats, little lookout posts hanging from corners and gatehouses guarding courtyards. As the years went on, these details became decorative rather than functional.

## Half-timbering

Though it is common all over Europe, the Normans were particularly adept at half-timbering. Using an early form of pre-fabrication, frames could be assembled on the ground and then hauled up into position. They were often dismantled and reassembled if and when the owner decided to build on or move. The timber beams of the framework (*pans de bois*) were filled in with wattle and daub (*hourdis*). Abundant local clay was often mixed with chopped straw or even cowdung

for extra strength. The wood itself has lasted for centuries because it was properly cut and aged. Felled in late autumn or winter, the day after a full moon so that sap levels were right, the timber was left to dry out slowly.

Facing page: granite farmhouse near Avranches
Above: typical half-timbered manor house in the Pays d'Auge
Below: in Beuvron-en-Auge

## Cabourg

Popular with families, this resort on the Côte Fleurie boasts a 3-km (2-mile) promenade. Once a simple fishing village, in 1860 it was redeveloped with streets radiating out from the Grand Hôtel and casino. Many *belle époque* buildings survive but Cabourg is best known as Marcel Proust's childhood holiday destination, renamed 'Balbec' in his novel *À l'Ombre des Jeunes Filles en Fleurs* (Within a Budding Grove). The annual Romantic Film Festival in June is great fun. *On the coast, 22km (14 miles) northeast of Caen.*

## Camembert

The village is not much more than a church, a few houses and a famous name. The Beaumoncel farm, perched overlooking the church, is where Marie Harel developed the famous cheese; its owners open the farm for tours in summer. Down in the village, a cheese-box-shaped visitors' centre and a museum aim for the coach tourist market and push the products of a dairy conglomerate on the gift-shop shelves. Follow road signs to the town's only farmer-cheesemaker to get the real thing. *Manoir de Beaumoncel. Open: July–mid-Aug, daily, afternoons. 3km (2 miles) south of Vimoutiers, on the D246.*

## Château du Champ-de-Bataille

Parisian owner Jacques Garcia spent two years restoring this late 17th-century mansion château, reopening it in 1994. Admire the marble, tapestries and paintings, then stroll through the woods and parkland. *37km (23 miles) southwest of Rouen, off the D840. Tel: 02 32 34 84 34. Open: Mar–May & mid-Sept–mid-Nov, Sat & Sun; May–mid-Sept, daily. Admission charge.*

## Clécy

If you want to take a break from history, abbeys and châteaux, Clécy, in the heart of the Suisse Normande by the River Orne, is a centre for walking, canoeing, rock-climbing and hang-gliding.

## Musée du Chemin de Fer Miniature (Model Railway Museum)

Children and fans of model trains enjoy

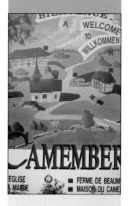

### MARIE HAREL

A priest fleeing the Revolutionary mob took refuge in the village of Camembert. In gratitude, he gave 'his' recipe for a Brie-like cheese to his protector, the farmer's wife Marie Harel.

She and her daughter (also Marie) improved and refined it; a grandson gained recognition when Napoleon III approved of the flavour and ordered more in the 1850s. That is the legend; but Camembert only became famous after M. Ridel invented the circular chipwood box in 1890, enabling the cheeses to be shipped in quantity. Marie gets all the credit, however . . . and two statues in Vimoutiers.

'Europe's largest miniature railway layout' with an airport and coal mine. There are some 180 locomotives and 500 trucks plus a short model train ride in the grounds.

*Les Fours à Chaux. Tel: 02 31 69 07 13. Open: Apr–Oct, daily; winter, Sun afternoons only (see pp186–7). Admission charge.*

*Clécy is 38km (23$^1$/2 miles) southeast of Caen, on the D562.*

## Conches-en-Ouche

This is another 'ordinary' Norman town with one of everything. In the 16th-century Church of Ste-Foy, which occupies the site of a church founded by Roger de Tosny after the Crusades, look for the 'Mystic Wine Press' in the fifth window in the south aisle. For atmosphere, visit the crumbling, overgrown ruins of the castle keep, dramatically floodlit in summer. A museum of glass exhibits luminous objets d'art ancient and modern.

*18km (11 miles) southwest of Évreux, on the D830. Musée de Verre, Route de Sainte Marguerite. Tel: 02 32 30 90 41. Open: June–mid-Sept, Wed–Sat standard hours, Sun afternoons. Admission charge.*

## Château de Crèvecoeur-en-Auge

A stream meanders through manicured lawns surrounding an ochre and half-timbered manor house; geese and ducks splash in the water, children fish in the moat. It is all idyllic, except for the traffic whizzing by on the N13. This cluster of ancient buildings includes a chapel, gatehouse and dovecote.

The current owners made a fortune from their technique of using seismology to search for oil back in 1927. Today, a museum about oil prospecting is housed here and modern art exhibitions contrast with the story of medieval architecture. Numerous special events interpret medieval life and Norman rural traditions; check website or call for schedule.

*www.chateau-de-crevecoeur.com 34km (21 miles) east of Caen, on the N13. Museum tel: 02 31 63 02 45. Open: Mar–Sept, daily from late morning; Oct, Sun afternoons only. Admission charge.*

Demonstrating life in a fortified manor at Château de Crèvecoeur-en-Auge

### Deauville

Bette Davis, Elizabeth Taylor, Lee Marvin, Roger Moore, John Travolta . . . the roll call of names by the cabins on the *planches* (boardwalk) proves this is, and has been, one of the world's great resorts. Yet Deauville hits the headlines of the society pages for only 14 weeks each summer (*see pp154–5*).

History records that the half-brother of Napoleon III, the Duc de Morny, decided to develop the sand dunes to the west of Trouville, aiming to build a posher version of that holiday spot. That was in 1860. For making Deauville a magnet for society-types, however, credit goes to Eugène Cornuché. In 1910, he built a casino, a racecourse and the 700-m (2,297-ft) long boardwalk on the wide beach, so the rich and famous didn't have to get their shoes sandy.

In recent years, Deauville has worked hard to maintain its up-market image: a new marina at the mouth of the River Touques, more flowerbeds, repaved squares and an even longer boardwalk. Forget the semi-seediness of some seaside towns: here, buildings are strictly regulated to conform to the 'traditional' half-timbered Norman style, taking full advantage of the historical colour palette to lend a festive air. The 'cottages' facing the ocean are sized in medium, large and giant, like the sprawling Hôtel Normandy next to the casino. To experience the *joie de vivre* that makes Deauville legendary, visit during 'the season'. That's when the stars of the gossip columns are shopping in the jewellers' and designer boutiques. Out of season, the shutters of houses and apartments behind the seafront are firmly closed and the atmosphere is muted, but there are bargains, even at the priciest hotels. Deauville attracts visitors all year long; even in winter, a fine weekend brings promenaders to the boardwalk and champagne-sippers to the Bar du Soleil.

*61km (38 miles) northeast of Caen, on the coast.*

### Dives-sur-Mer

From here William of Normandy set off to conquer England in 1066. The names of 475 of the warriors who assembled here are on the west wall of the touchingly decrepit church of Notre-Dame in what is now just an ordinary seaside village. Look for the lepers' hole in the right-hand wall.

*22km (14 miles) northeast of Caen, on the coast.*

The new marina at Deauville

Colourful corner in Dives-sur-Mer

## Dreux

Dreux is busy but rather soulless, except for the pedestrianised streets in the old centre with its 16th-century belfry. The castle here was pulled down in 1593 for choosing the 'wrong' side against Henri IV. Dreux had already been given to the royal Orléans family, which explains the tombs of exiled King Louis-Philippe and family in the early 19th-century Chapelle Royale St Louis above the town.
*80km (50 miles) west of Paris, on the N12.*

## Ecouis

In the Church of Notre-Dame, classical music echoes from speakers under the brick-vaulted ceiling. Among the notable carved and painted wood panelling and statues is a 14th-century statue of St Agnes wearing a pleated gown worthy of the couturier Fortuny. Find it on the northwest wall of the transept. Realistic carvings on the choir stalls include an old man's head on a rat's body. Well worth a stop.
*Off the D321 west of Fleury. Tel: 02 32 69 43 08. Open: daily. Admission charge.*

The **Abbaye de Fontaine-Guérard**, a tranquil 12th-century ruin on the River Andelle, is quite haunting at dusk.
*37km (23 miles) southeast of Rouen, on the N14.*

## Évreux

The ancient capital of the Eure is mainly modern, with factories on the outskirts but river-side walks and flowerbeds in the centre. Ransacked, besieged and bombarded for over 1,000 years, the few survivors of the past include the Tour de l'Horloge, a medieval clock tower whose two-tonne bell is known as Louise, the Cathédrale de Notre-Dame, topped by the Clocher d'Argent (silver bell tower), and the Ancien Évêché (Old Bishop's Palace).
*53km (33 miles) south of Rouen, on the N154.*

15th-century stained glass at Évreux Cathedral

## Falaise

The Dukes of Normandy owned castles and land all over the region, so many towns and villages can justifiably claim links with the best known of the dynasty – William the Conqueror. It is William's birthplace, Falaise, where he is most celebrated. William's birth, in 1027, was not particularly auspicious (*see box*) and though the town's castle was not completed until more than 200 years after his death, William would have been proud of the massive edifice, with its 29 towers. The castle was rebuilt after being severely damaged in August 1944 during bitter fighting, when the Allied forces encountered strong German resistance. Further extensive restoration was completed in 1994.

The castle now houses a spectacular audiovisual display telling the story of the Anglo-Norman kings. You can also climb the battlements and gaze out from the window in the Chambre d'Arlette, from where Duke William's father supposedly spotted the tanner's daughter. In the town, the square is dominated by a statue of William on his charger, while two contrasting museums describe the battle for the Falaise Pocket in 1944 and house a delightful

Stern sentinel – Falaise Castle stands on a great bluff over the valley

### THE DUKE AND THE TANNER'S DAUGHTER

Arlette, the beautiful daughter of a Falaise tanner, caught the eye of the Duke of Normandy while she was washing clothes. Some say he was standing in the 'Chambre d'Arlette' in the castle, but the plaque at the Vieux Lavoir maintains he was returning from a hunt. Both versions agree that the offer was 'mistress, not marriage'. She accepted, and her son, William the Bastard, became King of England.

### BOUDIN (1824–98)

Born in Honfleur, Eugène Boudin was nicknamed *le Roi des Ciels* (the King of the Skies) by Courbet for his stirring seascapes. But it was his constant striving to capture light that made him the modest precursor of the Impressionists. Honfleur honours his memory with a museum; the Ferme de St-Siméon, where he and the Impressionists painted, is now a luxury hotel.

collection of automata from the 1930s and 1940s, orginally seen in Parisian shop-window displays.

*35km (22 miles) south of Caen, on the N158. Château Guillaume le Conquerant tel: 02 31 41 61 44. Open: daily. Closed: Jan. Admission charge.*
*Musée Aout 1944: Chemin des Roches. Tel: 02 31 90 37 19. Open: Apr–mid-Nov, Wed–Mon. Admission charge.*
*Musée d'Automates: boulevard de la Liberation. Tel 02 31 90 02 43.*
*Open: Apr–Sept, daily. Admission charge.*

## Gisors

The revolutionary octagonal keep marked a breakthrough in military design back in 1097 when King William Rufus of England built it to defend the River Epte, Normandy's border with France. The castle is long gone but the keep remains atop its 20-m (66-ft) high hillock overlooking this pleasant town.
*57km (35 miles) southeast of Rouen, on the D14.*

## Honfleur

Cafés and art galleries in stone and half-timbered buildings cluster around a small harbour where nets hang out to dry and fishing boats chug in and out: Honfleur is almost too good to be true. No wonder artists like Boudin, Monet (*see opposite & p48*) and Courbet were inspired. The nearby oil refineries of Le Havre and the new Pont de Normandie bridge are forgotten when you stand by La Lieutenance, the remains of the fortified gate and still the port offices. Here, a plaque honours Samuel de Champlain, founder of Québec in 1608. Up the hill is the **Église Ste-Catherine**, France's oldest

Ferme de St-Siméon Hotel, Honfleur, which the Impressionists made their base

and largest wooden church, built by shipwrights like two upside-down boats, side-by-side. Its 18-m (59-ft) tall bell tower, the Clocher Ste-Catherine, stands apart, on top of the former bell-ringers' house. Off the Quai St-Étienne, the rue de la Ville leads to the 17th-century **Greniers à Sel** (salt warehouses), built with stones from the old ramparts. The magnificent wooden roofs once protected 10,000 tons of salt but now shelter concerts and exhibitions.

### Musée Eugène Boudin

Compare works by Honfleur-inspired 19th-century artists such as Boudin and Monet with contemporary local painters, then return to mundane life, with 19th-century Norman bonnets and household utensils.
*Rue Place Erik Satie. Tel: 02 31 89 54 00. Open: Wed–Mon, standard hours (see pp186–7). Closed: Oct–mid-Mar, weekday mornings. Admission charge.*

*26km (16 miles) southeast of Le Havre, on the coast.*

Basilique Ste-Thérèse, Lisieux, completed in the 1950s

### Houlgate

Houlgate's wide sandy beach was once favoured by the very rich, but this early seaside resort has faded in recent decades. To the east, the Vaches-Noires (black cows) are actually cliffs tumbling into the sea and are a favourite haunt for fossil collectors. At low tide, covered in seaweed, they look like sleepy ruminants.
*33km (20 miles) northeast of Caen, on the coast.*

### Lisieux

A million pilgrims come each year to the 93-m (305-ft) high white Byzantine basilica of Ste-Thérèse, one of the biggest churches built anywhere in the world in the 20th century. Deeply pious, Thérèse Martin (born in Alençon in 1873) joined the Carmelite nunnery here at the age of 15. She died nine years later and was made a saint in 1925. At the basilica,

pilgrims can see a film, attend a special Mass, view the waxworks and pray to her remains in the Carmelite chapel. Her house, Les Buissonets, is on boulevard Herbet-Fournet. Less religious visitors can enjoy the lively Saturday-morning market and the Cathédrale St-Pierre, an elegant example of 12th-century Gothic stonework.
*51km (32 miles) east of Caen, on the N13.*

### Livarot

This heartbreakingly tatty town gave its name to an assertive soft cheese, distinctive for its rings of marsh grass. The Graindorge factory, just on the southern edge of town, has a very informative self-guided factory visit, with tastings in the shop. For a more artisanal cheese, drive 9km (5¹/₂ miles) northwest to Boissey's Fromagers de Tradition, where morning cheesemaking can be seen through the workshop windows.
*18km (11 miles) southwest of Lisieux, on the D579. Fromagerie Graindorge. Tel: 02 31 48 20 10. Open: Mon–Fri & Sat mornings, standard hours (see pp186–7). Fromagers de Tradition, D4 in Boissey, follow sign in town to fromagerie. Open: Mon–Fri 9am–4pm for cheese sales.*

### Louviers

Despite damage in 1940, this town between Rouen and

Ste Thérèse is responsible for turning Lisieux into a miniature Lourdes

Évreux retains many charming half-timbered houses and a church as elaborate as a small cathedral. The River Eure splits into separate streams which helped develop the cloth industry between the 12th and 15th centuries. The tourist office is in the 16th-century home of the King's Jester.
*31km (19 miles) southeast of Rouen, off the A13.*

### Orbec

On the banks of the River Orbiquet, this is the kind of small town that visitors tend to bypass because it has no famous attraction, yet that is precisely its allure. Window-shop and admire the appealing old houses on the Grande Rue, where you are allowed inside the photo-worthy, 400-year-old Vieux Manoir, the local museum. The Église de Notre-Dame has a vast belfry, started as a defensive tower in the 15th century and given a more decorative finishing touch in the 16th.
*21km (13 miles) southeast of Lisieux, on the D519. Vieux Manoir, 107 rue Grande. Tel: 02 31 32 58 89. Open: July–Aug, Wed, Sat & Sun (Mon, Thur & Fri, afternoons only); Easter–Christmas, Wed, Sat & Sun, afternoons.*

### Ouistreham/Riva-Bella

Summer brings families to the wide-open, breezy beaches and promenade; the ferry to England brings cars and returning Britons all year round. This small resort's claim to fame came on D-Day in 1944 when the left flank of the Allies' attack landed here.
*On the coast, 14km (9 miles) north of Caen, on the D514.*

### Pegasus Bridge

The bridge over the River Orne north of Caen was a vital D-Day target. The café alongside was the first house liberated in France and still sees emotional reunions every 6 June. The name Pegasus Bridge came from the emblem of the Parachute Regiment. The bridge was removed in 1993, but is on public view as part of a 12,000-sq m (129,167-sq ft) park, which also includes a D-Day museum.
*Memorial Pegasus, Ranville, 8km (5 miles) north of Caen, off the D514. Tel: 02 31 78 19 44; www.normandy1944.com Open: Feb–Nov, daily. Admission charge.*

### Pont-l'Évêque

Another town with a famous cheese, Pont-l'Évêque dates back at least 700 years. It straddles three rivers, the Calonne, Yvie and Touques. Despite considerable damage in World War II, there are still many fine half-timbered houses. The courtyard of the Aigle d'Or coaching inn at 68 rue de Vaucelles is worth a look.
*47km (29 miles) northeast of Caen, off the A13.*

First for freedom: the café at Pegasus Bridge

### Château de St-Germain-de-Livet

Just outside Lisieux, this moated mansion demands a stop. White stone, pink brick, and glazed green brick combine in an unusual and eye-catching chequerboard façade dating from the 16th century. Inside, splendid late 16th-century frescoes of biblical scenes decorate the Guards' Room.
*Tel: 02 31 31 00 03. Open: Wed–Mon, standard hours (see pp186–7). Closed: Dec & Jan.*

### St-Pierre-sur-Dives

Don't miss the enormous covered market here. After it was burnt down in 1944, restoration of the huge beams (joined only by chestnut pegs) followed original plans, so that the 900-year-old heart of the community was revived for the sale of fruit and vegetables (Mondays) and a monthly sale of antiques and bric-a-brac. A nearby bar, the Greenwich, refers to the line across the floor in the old Benedictine abbey church; at midday, the sun shines along it through a plaque in the window. There is also a museum focusing on cheese-making techniques.
*27km (17 miles) southeast of Caen, on the D40.*

### Château de Vendeuvre

A collection of miniature furniture. Many pieces are inlaid with metal or ivory; some were executed as test pieces for full membership of a guild. Look for the tiny cupboard containing a craftsman's minuscule tools.
*6km (4 miles) southwest of St-Pierre on the D271. Tel: 02 31 40 93 83. Open: May–Sept, daily; Apr, Oct, Nov, Sun &*

If you like 'kiss-me-quick' resorts, you'll love Trouville-sur-Mer

*holiday afternoons. Closed: Nov–mid-Mar.*

### Sword Beach

This was the easternmost British sector of the D-Day landings (*see pp66–9*).

### Thury-Harcourt

This rebuilt town on the River Orne is a pleasant place for relaxing. The northern gateway to the Suisse Normande (*see p6*), it makes a good base for walking, canoeing on the river, riding and cycling.
*27km (17 miles) south of Caen, on the D562.*

### Trouville-sur-Mer

Where Deauville is sophisticated, Trouville is jolly and down-to-earth, with its fishing port and quayside stalls for the catch. In fact, Trouville triggered France's sea-bathing boom 150 years ago when writers Alexandre Dumas and Gustave Flaubert sang its praises. Families stroll round the harbour and, when rain threatens, head for the Aquarium (*see* Children *p159*).

## Musée Montebello

Scenes of sailors, the beach and the harbour are among paintings of 19th-century Trouville by Boudin (*see p78*) and local talents. Amusing depictions of the early days of sea-bathing, complete with pyjama-like costumes.
*64 rue du Général Leclerc.*
*Tel: 02 31 88 16 26. Open: Apr–Sept, Wed–Mon, afternoons (see pp186–7). Admission charge.*

*Trouville is situated on the opposite bank of the River Touques to Deauville.*

## Verneuil-sur-Avre

Verneuil is a pretty town with pleasant old streets (rue du Canon, rue de la Madeleine), a moat and two unusual historic remains. The 60-m (197-ft) tall tower of the Madeleine church recalls Rouen Cathedral's Tour de Beurre, so-called because it was built with the donations of penitents who had eaten butter during Lent. The nearby Tour Grise (grey tower) is a 13th-century keep built of reddish stone.
*36km (22 miles) west of Dreux, on the N12.*

## Vimoutiers

This larger neighbour of Camembert gave the cheese its introduction to the world, as the nearest market town. One statue of its 'inventor', Marie Harel, stands in the plain main square; another, by the church, was decapitated when the town was razed in June 1944. In the Place facing the church, a cauldron sits memorialised for its role in feeding the town that trying summer. A small **museum** in the tourist office has one-legged milkstools, labels, copper churns, and a multilingual video all about the local product.
*27km (17 miles) south of Lisieux, on the D579. Musée du Camembert: 10 avenue Général de Gaulle. Tel: 02 33 39 30 29. Open: Mar–Oct, standard hours (see pp186–7).*

Antiques fair in the must-see barn at St Pierre-sur-Dives

Say 'Normandy' and most people think of 'apples'. This fruit appears with chicken and pork, alongside *boudin* (black pudding), or stuffed into the *gâteau de Trouville* (an apple and cream cake). An apple baked in pastry is a *bourdelot* or *rabote*.

## Cider

Back in the 8th century, the Emperor Charlemagne supposedly encouraged his subjects to imbibe Normandy cider. Sadly, cider consumption has dropped dramatically, and the EU has even subsidised the uprooting of orchards to reduce surpluses of this refreshing light drink. Labels say *doux* (sweet) or *sec/brut* (dry), and proper cider (*bon bère*) must be at least 5 per cent alcohol according to law (a weaker version has about 3.5 per cent alcohol). Even without fluent French, it's fun to stop for a *dégustation* (tasting) at farms that produce the brew. Around Cambremer, southeast of Caen, signs proclaim *Cru de Cambremer* (grown in Cambremer, vintage Cambremer) which locals boast is the best (*see pp86–7*). Cider is traditionally served in pottery jugs, but be careful with *cidre bouché,* cider bottled with a Champagne-like cork. This sparkling version can be explosive if left in the back of a hot car.

## Calvados

Distil cider and you get calvados. The Normans learned how, 400 years ago, from their neighbours on the Loire, but it was only in the 19th century that standards were set at today's high level.

Abundantly grown, apples and pears are made into cider, calvados or perry, and also baked into mouth-watering desserts

Strict rules must be followed to receive the AOC (Appellation d'Origine Contrôlée) stamp of approval. By adding a little yeast, the mashed-up apples are fermented; the resulting liquid is distilled twice, often in glowing copper alembics. After maturation in oak casks for five to ten years, special committees taste it before certificating it for sale. Some calvados is aged for 30 years in white bottles labelled Hors d'Âge (ageless) and connoisseurs rate the best an equal to the finest cognac.

### The Norman hole

The legendary *trou Normand*, a shot of 'calva' drunk part way through a meal, drills a hole to make way for more food. Nowadays, a calvados-flavoured sorbet serves the purpose in some restaurants.

### Pommeau

This chilled cocktail is two parts apple *moût* (must, juice), one part calvados. Beware: it slips down all too easily, but packs a punch. It is often drunk as an aperitif.

### The pear

A pear baked in pastry is a *douillon*, and around Domfront the small, hard fruit is crushed and mashed like apples for a fruity, sparkling *poiré* (perry) – nothing like the bland, sweet liquid sold as perry in Britain.

# By bike: cider country

Normandy's small lanes are excellent for cyclists, although the lack of signposts can be a hazard, particularly if you stop for *dégustations* (tastings). This route follows part of the well-marked Route du Cidre (cider trail) through the lovely Auge Valley (17km/10 1/2 miles). The best producers are indicated by the Cru de Cambremer signs.

*Allow 2 to 3 hours.*

*Start in Cambremer.*

## 1 Cambremer

This village has a small information

centre on the place de l'Église, with its pretty parish church topped by a surprisingly large 11th-century tower. A festival celebrating all of Normandy's

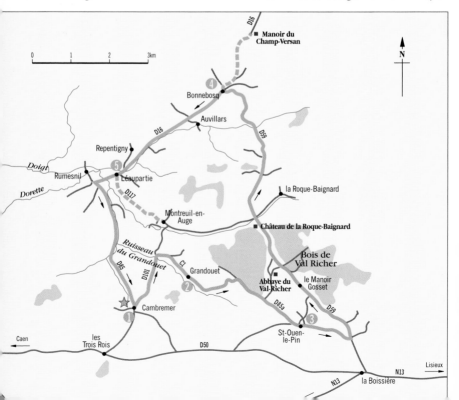

AOC foods – with plenty of tastings – is held the first weekend in May. In July, August and Easter week the town hosts a folksy market with many local foods. *Take the D101 signed la Roque-Baignard, following the Route du Cidre sign. Cross the Ruisseau du Grandouet. Turn right on to the C1. It is 1km (²/₃ mile) to Grandouet.*

## 2 Grandouet
This hamlet has a charming small church across from which is the bucolic Manoir du Grandouet, with tastings of its prize-winning Calva, cider and *poiré*. *Continue up the hill, rejoining the D85a. Turn right. Pedal past fields and woods. At a T-junction, turn left towards la Boissière and enter St-Ouen-le-Pin.*

## 3 St-Ouen-le-Pin
André Gide, who won the Nobel prize for literature in 1947, was mayor of this straggling village in his younger days. The 19th-century diplomat François Guizot, author of histories of the English Revolution and of European civilisation, is buried here.

Even if you don't particularly like cider you will enjoy cycling this route

*At the crossroads, turn left on the D59 to Bonnebosq and re-enter St-Ouen-le-Pin. In a small house on the right, another cider-maker, Michel Lesufleur, offers* dégustations. *The road to Bonnebosq is a pretty run past a stream and pond. Look left for the 17th-century Abbaye du Val-Richer (Abbey of Val Richer) where Guizot lived his later years (not open to the public). Another splendid private residence on the left, complete with moat, is the Château de la Roque-Baignard.*

## 4 Bonnebosq
If there is time, the peaceful, little-visited 16th-century Manoir du Champ-Versan, a few minutes along the D16, is worth a detour to see the huge fireplaces (*tel: 02 31 65 11 07; open: Easter to October, daily, afternoons; closed Mon and Tues, also Mon in July and Aug*). *On leaving Bonnebosq, turn off the Route du Cidre and left almost immediately on to the D16 to Léaupartie.*

## 5 Léaupartie
Locals boast that their *mairie* is the smallest in France but they are also proud of the famous stud. Energetic cyclists can take a detour on the D117 to Montreuil-en-Auge. A few minutes away is the Vieille Auberge. This century-old inn is popular with cyclists, who stop for refreshment while exploring the lanes and tasting home-produced cider. *Back in Léaupartie, turn left on to the D85 to Cambremer. Cycle through orchards that are full of blossom in spring. In autumn, hessian sacks stand bulging with apples. As you re-enter Cambremer, on the left, M. Forcher is another well-known cider producer. Return to the church.*

# Tour: cheese country

Normandy's fame for cheese depends on its rich pastures. This drive through the Pays d'Auge follows narrow lanes through cosy valleys and past small fields bordered by hedges. It also takes in tiny villages and historic relics.
*Allow 2 hours.*

*Start in Vimoutiers.*

## 1 Vimoutiers

The Camembert museum (in the tourist office) is an appropriate starting point. Drive up the hill towards the church. Beside the road is the original statue of Marie Harel (*see p74*). Erected in 1928, it was decapitated in World War II

bombing. Its svelte replacement stands in the town centre.
*Turn left on the D916 then bear left on the D16 towards Camembert. At the bottom of the hill, turn right on the D246 to Camembert, past wayside farms. A huge cross on the left stands opposite a stone stele dedicated to Marie Harel. Continue straight on for the time being,*

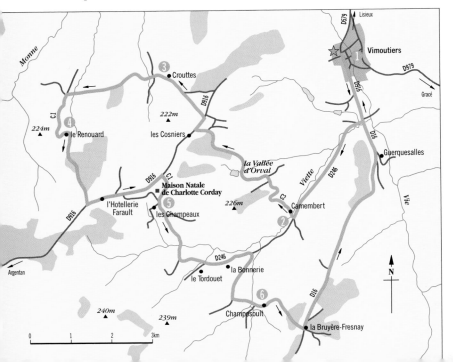

*following signs to Ferme de la Héronniére, just a couple of minutes down the road, for a farm and fromagerie tour and sampling of the last farmer-made AOC camembert in France (tel: 02 33 39 08 08). Take the right turn which leads across a bridge and up the hill.*

## 2 Camembert

In this hamlet, the modern Maison du Camembert faces the 16th-century manor house of Beaumoncel, where the legendary recipe was developed.

*Continue over the hill on the C2, a single-track road. Halfway down, bear left at a T-junction into the valley of the River Orval. At the main road, the D916, turn right, back towards Vimoutiers. Turn left soon, next to a small modern cottage on an unmarked side road to Crouttes.*

## 3 Crouttes

It is easy to spot the spire of the church where Marie Harel was baptised in 1761. The Prieuré St-Michel beyond, with its 13th-century chapel and granary, is now a centre for arts and crafts (*tel: 02 33 39 15 15. Open: May–Sept, daily, afternoons. Free admission*).

*Leave Crouttes. Halfway up the hill, turn left on to the C1 for le Renouard, going up a lane marked 'Église'. (If you reach the brick schoolhouse and* mairie *(town hall), you've gone too far.)*

## 4 Le Renouard

Look across the valley to the church of le Renouard and a remarkable fortified manor house with restored stone tower, arches and half-timbering. Past the church, the road wriggles through woods.

*Back at the D916, turn left towards Vimoutiers. Take the abrupt right on to the C1 to les Champeaux and Maison Natale de Charlotte Corday.*

## 5 Maison Natale de Charlotte Corday

The young noblewoman, Charlotte Corday, is remembered for stabbing Jacobin politician Marat in his bath in 1793. A descendant of the 17th-century playwright Corneille, Corday was born in this small Norman farmhouse (on the left, not open to the public).

*Continue past the Église des Lignerits, the church where Corday was baptised. Turn left at the T-junction, and left again on to the D246. There are several fine stud farms here. Just after the Haras de la Bonnerie, turn sharply right towards Champosoult.*

## 6 Champosoult

Champosoult is where Marie Harel lived and died. The old house is not open to the public; her tomb is in the graveyard.

*Continue to la Bruyère-Fresnay, whose modern church contrasts with the ancient Norman style. Then rejoin the main road, the D16, and return to Vimoutiers.*

The finest cheese bought fresh from the maker

The famed beaches of Normandy

# Western Normandy

This region boasts two of the best-known sights in France: Mont-St-Michel and the Bayeux Tapestry. One is a triumph of grand-scale engineering, the other a masterpiece of the minute: both attract visitors from all over the world. Then there are the beaches of D-Day, 6 June 1944. The older generation come to remember and pay their respects to fallen comrades, the younger to learn just how dangerous and difficult the Allied invasion actually was.

From Ouistreham (in Central Normandy) to Ste-Mère-Église, via Courseulles, Arromanches and Utah Beach, the coast is fringed with unattractive modern cottages and hotels. Mainly flat and open, these beaches would hold little attraction were it not for this famous moment in history.

The upthrust of the Contentin peninsula presents a different Normandy: tall, dark cliffs, grey stone villages, and a sense of remoteness. Cherbourg, dominated by a hilltop fortress, is

Le Mont-St-Michel

undergoing a face-lift to pretty up its rugged image as a naval base. Bollards along the Voie de la Liberté mark the 1,145-km (711-mile) Liberty Road (from the Cotentin to Bastogne in Belgium) beginning with '0' at Ste-Mère-Église and '00' at Utah Beach.

The west coast of the peninsula is dramatic (*see pp100–101*) but there are also seaside resorts like Barneville-Carteret and Granville, where families can swim in the clean, if cold, waters straight from the Atlantic.

Inland, the countryside is full of the unexpected. Coutances and Avranches have imposing churches that seem overlarge for these towns, while in Valognes, the market square and 18th-century mansions are surprisingly grand. Lessay's annual fair brings some 250,000 visitors to look at domestic livestock.

Villedieu-les-Poêles has a tradition of metalwork, from copper *poêles* (frying pans) to pewter and even bells, still cast at a cobwebbed foundry. Some souvenirs may have a tacky shine, but don't be put off: there is high-quality cookware on offer, too. Similarly, imports from elsewhere often overshadow the well-made, traditional pottery of Noron-la-Poterie near Bayeux.

Here and there are abbeys that have succumbed to time and the French Revolution. Cérisy has lost most of its nave, though long stretches of back-breakingly-built stone walls still edge the monastery's land, while white-painted fences, on the other hand, signpost stud farms. The Haras at St-Lô is one of France's best-known national studs.

## Western Normandy

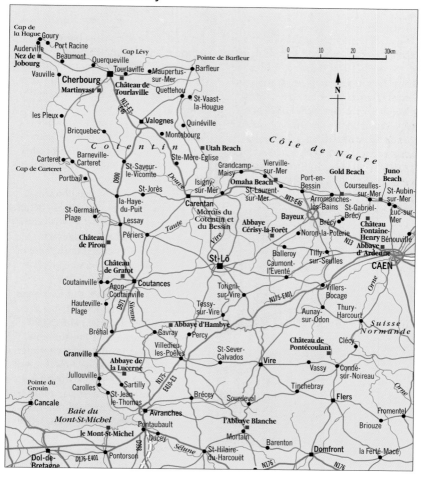

# Bayeux

'We've seen the tapestry, so what else is there?' Bayeux has worked hard in recent years to live up to the fame of 'the Conquest Hanging', as it used to be called. First came the Centre Guillaume le Conquérant to properly display and explain La Tapisserie, then the new Musée Mémorial de la Bataille de Normandie 1944.

The central tower of
Bayeux Cathedral

The town itself, with cobbled streets and historic houses, escaped serious damage in the post-D-Day fighting, thanks to Dom Aubourg, a chaplain at St-Vigor's Priory. Having convinced the Allied troops that the Germans had fled, his reward was seeing the *tricolore* raised on 7 June over the first liberated city in France.

There is more to its history, however, than 1066 and 1944. In 905, Bayeux

Even large houses in Bayeux are half-timbered

became the 'cradle of the Norman Empire' when a son was born to the daughter of the governor and the Viking leader, Rollo, later first Duke of Normandy. Unfortunately, William the Conqueror had no sentimental feeling later on and sacked the town while suppressing rebellious barons; later, its cathedral was built by his half-brother, Bishop Odo, with profits from the invasion of England.

In the Middle Ages, neighbouring Caen grew in power and Bayeux became a backwater. Lahaeudrie, a 19th-century historian, wrote that '. . . the town remains . . . veiled in an atmosphere of soothing melancholy mingled with a powerful feeling of the past.'

That sense of history is today's great attraction. Street names still read like a shopping directory: rue Laitière (for buying milk), rue de la Poissonnerie (the fishmarket) and rue des Cuisiniers (the cooks). Rue Franche, however, was named by St-Manvieu; having brought an infant back to life as it was about to be buried, the saint ordered that no one doomed to die should use Franche, or Free Street.

The town's oldest house, a classic of medieval half-timbering (formerly the

# Bayeux

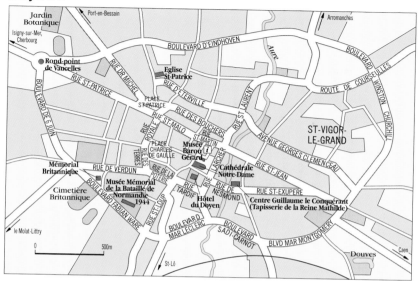

tourist office), is on rue St-Martin, opposite the 18th-century Maison du Cadran, decorated with a sundial and a 'month' dial. Look along the tiny side streets towards the cathedral for glimpses of its tower and spires; admire the 18th-century *hôtels* (town mansions) built of pale stone behind elaborate gates. Look in the courtyard behind the cathedral for the town's magnificent Liberty Tree, planted in the heady days of Revolution. The centre of Bayeux is small but full of charm.

## Cathédrale Notre-Dame

The Bayeux Tapestry was displayed on special days in the cathedral, where 'improvements' over the centuries include the copper 'bonnet' on the lantern tower, dating from the 19th century. Yet the look is essentially Norman: over 100m (330ft) long and 22m (73ft) high, with

rounded arches decorated with Scandinavian and Anglo-Saxon designs. Spot the monsters and monkeys cavorting in the carved 'basketwork' pattern. *Place des Tribunaux.*

View along the length of the cathedral nave during Sunday-morning Mass

Tapestry reproduction in Bayeux Cathedral

**Tapisserie de Bayeux (Bayeux Tapestry)**
'Item, a very long piece of cloth embroidered with pictures and inscriptions representing the conquest of England . . .' That listing in the 1476 inventory of Bayeux Cathedral refers to one of the most famous pieces of sewing in the world. As simple as a strip cartoon, it portrays the events leading up to and including the Battle of Hastings, where William of Normandy defeated King Harold of England. Legend has it that Queen Matilda and her ladies-in-waiting stitched the embroidery. Historians surmise that monks produced it by sewing wool on linen on the orders of Odo, Bishop of Bayeux, William's half-brother. The tapestry would have been exhibited for the first time when Bayeux Cathedral was dedicated in 1077, in William's presence. But is this an historical record or 11th-century Norman propaganda? Work your way through the various exhibitions, listen to the headset, study the tapestry and then decide for yourself.

**Salle Guillaume**
Supported by music and slides, which are projected on to a fleet of white 'sails', the story of the Danish invasions of western Europe is told. An exhibition expands the story of the tapestry and shows how William stamped his authority on England after 1066.

**Salle Mathilde**
Maps place the toings and froings across the English Channel in context, and an excellent 14-minute film (alternate showings in French and English) tells the tale of William's life. It unravels the political machinations leading to the invasion and focuses on the tapestry in detail.

**The Tapestry**
It is not a series of huge wall hangings but a long, narrow cloth (70m by 0.5m/230ft by 1$\frac{1}{2}$ft) with 'almost juvenile stitching' in rust red, moss green and slate blue. Some panels show static figures, others have plenty of action, with horses trotting and pulling on the reins. Look in the borders for rude drawings and grotesque animals, the needlework equivalent of gargoyles. The Tapestry has 58 panels. These are some of the key scenes to watch out for.

**Panel 23:** Harold swears the oath of allegiance to William, touching the Gospels and a holy relic. This is the basis of William's claim to the English throne.

**Panel 26:** The body of King Edward the Confessor is carried to Westminster

Abbey. Note the two small figures with funeral bells; also, the hand of God stretching down from heaven.

**Panels 32 and 33:** Harold has been crowned king but a comet foretells doom. In the lower border, five boats predict the invasion of England.

**Panels 37 and 38:** Crossing the English Channel: first, casks of wine, suits of chain mail, swords and axes are loaded; then a stiff wind catches the sails; finally, the horses are led off and the boats pulled up on shore.

**Panels 42 and 43:** Note the spit-roasted chickens and kebabs, served up at a banquet.

**Panels 40 and 47:** Separated by the feast, these panels show the invaders stealing sheep, cattle and plate, then setting fire to a house, leaving a mother and child homeless.

**Panel 48:** Mounted soldiers in silver-thread chain mail charge into battle, lances at the ready. William and his half-brother, Bishop Odo, however, carry maces.

The following scenes are full of detail, from delicately stitched arrows to the horror of upended horses, decapitated bodies and hand-to-hand combat.

**Panel 55:** Rumour has it that William is dead; lifting his visor, he rallies his troops before the final assault.

**Panel 57:** A golden arrow pierces Harold's eye and skull, killing him. After 14 hours, the battle is over. On 14 October, 1066, William of Normandy is King of England.

*Centre Guillaume le Conquérant, rue de Nesmond. Tel: 02 31 51 25 50.*
*Open: daily. Admission charge; a special ticket covers this plus the three smaller museums in Bayeux.*

Bayeux Cathedral's lace-work towers in the old city

## Musée Baron Gérard

This fine, small museum's eclectic collection ranges from old pharmacy bottles to a 17th-century cabinet that is a *tour de force* of marquetry. Most interesting are displays of local porcelain, pottery and lace. Apple blossom and forget-me-nots decorate 19th-century Bayeux porcelain, whose slight blue tinge typifies china clay from the Manche. Salt glaze, on the other hand, produces the bluish lustre of the pottery (*see p106*), still made in nearby Noron-la-Poterie. Examples of local lace justify its renown, especially the black, with a shadow effect, and the '*blonde*' (ivory silk). In Bayeux, *fuseaux* (spindles) were used; note the personalised set from 1840: '*je suis de Victorine*'.

*Place de la Liberté. Tel: 02 31 92 14 21. Open: daily, standard hours (see pp186–7). Admission charge.*

## Musée Diocésain d'Art Religieux and Conservatoire de la Dentelle de Bayeux (Hôtel du Doyen)

The lace-making school is fascinating. Here women carry on the town's proud tradition in the Hôtel du Doyen. By comparison, the collection of religious art is dull.

*6 Rue Lambert-Leforestier. Tel: 02 31 92 14 21/73 80. Open: daily, standard hours (see pp186–7). Admission charge.*

## Musée Mémorial de la Bataille de Normandie 1944

This museum, tracing the 76-day Battle of Normandy, is one of the best of its kind. Covering the build-up as well as the action, the foot soldiers as well as the major players, the museum appeals to children as well as to veterans. Newspapers of the day are juxtaposed with propaganda leaflets; a 'letter to Mom' is next to a Purple Heart, the American

Inside the Château de Balleroy

military medal. A diorama, complete with rubble, shows Poles and Americans meeting up on 19 August 1944, and a film (French and English) tells the story, with original footage.
*Boulevard Fabian Ware. Tel: 02 31 51 46 90. Open: daily, standard hours (see pp186–7). Admission charge.*

### Arromanches-les-Bains
A Mulberry Harbour, made in England and floated across the Channel, allowed 2½ million soldiers, half a million vehicles and 4 million tons of equipment to land in the 100 days after D-Day. At low tide, remnants of the half-million tons of concrete linked by 16km (10 miles) of steel 'roads' are visible. *Arromanches 360* is an 18-minute film which recreates the event.
*Chemin du Calvaire. Tel: 02 31 22 30 30; www.arromanches360.com.*
*Open: daily. Closed: Jan. Admission charge.*

### Musée du Débarquement
Dioramas, models, films and photographs recall the historic dawn of 6 June 1944 in a museum on the beach itself.
*Tel: 02 31 22 34 31. Open: daily, standard hours (see pp186–7). Closed: Jan. Admission charge.*

*Arromanches is on the coast, 31km (19 miles) northwest of Caen.*

### Avranches
In the 8th century, St Aubert, Bishop of Avranches, foolishly disregarded two visions of St Michael ordering him to build a chapel. The third time, the archangel poked his *doigt de feu* (fiery finger) in the bishop's skull . . . and

Mont-St-Michel was then built. There are splendid views of it from the Jardin des Plantes, while the bishop's perforated pate is in the treasury of the Basilica of St Gervais. Illuminated manuscripts from Mont-St-Michel are displayed in summer in the Town Hall.

At the west end of the Bishop's Palace is the square Thomas à Becket, where a stone tablet marks the spot where King Henry II of England did penance and received papal absolution in 1172 for involvement in the murder of Thomas à Becket. The Place Patton commemorates General Patton's 1944 success against the German counter-attack from the Mortain pocket.
*100km (62 miles) southwest of Caen, off the N175.*

### Château de Balleroy
This haughty 17th-century pink and grey mansion stares down its avenue straight into the village. In the Waterloo Room, portraits of Napoleon and the Duke of Wellington glower at one another across the fireplace. It is owned by the family of the late Malcolm Forbes, the American magazine publisher. A balloon enthusiast, his museum portrays ballooning from Montgolfier in 1783 to the barrage balloons of World War II.
*15km (9 miles) southwest of Bayeux, off the D572.*
*Tel: 02 31 21 60 61. Open: daily. Closed: Oct–Mar, Sat & Sun. Admission charge.*

### Barenton
The Maison de la Pomme et de la Poire tells the story of cider and calvados as well

Mussel pickers at Barfleur; the lighthouse is visible in the distance

as of the varieties of apples and pears in the orchards surrounding this old farm.
*10km (6 miles) southeast of Mortain, on the D907. Tel: 02 33 59 56 22. Open: Apr–end Sept, daily, standard hours (see pp186–7). Admission charge.*

### Barfleur

A charming harbour full of fishing boats faced by granite cottages with stone roofs, Barfleur has its fair share of sailors' tales: William the Conqueror's boat, the *Mora*, was built here; later, in 1120, the *Blanche Nef* (White Ship) sank in the fierce offshore currents, with 300 noblemen and King Henry I of England's only son, William, aboard. In 1194, King Richard the Lionheart sailed back to England from here after his release from captivity in Austria. Barfleur claims France's first lifeboat station (1865) and one of the

tallest lighthouses, the phare de Gatteville. Climb one step for each day of the year to reach the fabulous view from 74.85m (246ft) up.
*27km (17 miles) east of Cherbourg, on the D901. Phare de Gatteville, 5km (3 miles) north of Barfleur (D116 then D10). Tel: 02 33 23 17 97. Open: daily, weather and duties permitting. Closed: mid-Nov–Jan. Modest admission charge.*

### Barneville-Carteret

Since 1965, three villages have become one: Carteret, a commercial harbour, Barneville, the old inland village, and Barneville-Plage, the newer resort and marina. The rocky Cap de Carteret protects a curving bay which has a sandy nature reserve set on dunes on the far side of the Gerfleur estuary. Legend says that the Channel Islands were separated from mainland France in 709 by a tidal wave. This is one of the most popular family resorts on the Cotentin Peninsula.
*On the coast, 38km (24 miles) southwest of Cherbourg, via the D904.*

### Cérisy-la-Forêt, Abbaye

The main road from Bayeux to St-Lô cuts through the beech forest of Cérisy; turn off for the tranquil Romanesque abbey which would have been awesome 800 years ago. Now, even though a large slice of its nave is missing, it is imposing, with three tiers of windows in

Plaque in Barfleur showing William's ship

the chancel, plus a square tower and spire soaring above the 15th-century choir stalls.

*Tel: 02 33 56 12 15. Open: Easter–mid-Nov, daily. Guided tours available. Admission charge for guided tour.*

## Cherbourg

Over a million ferry passengers a year stream through this port; now Cherbourg is sprucing up its image, hoping to tempt them to linger. A new *gare maritime* (ferry terminal) has been built, the Chantereyne marina has opened near the French navy's nuclear submarine base, and the former fish market has been replaced by a smart indoor market and leisure centre. Trees have been planted along quaysides, cafés spill on to pavements, and old houses are being renovated. The 1963 film, *Les Parapluies de Cherbourg* (*The Umbrellas of Cherbourg*) was re-released in 1992, tempting a new generation of Catherine Deneuve fans to seek out the umbrella shop in the rue du Port.

## Musée Thomas-Henry

This art collection includes works by native son Jean-François Millet, born in 1814 at Gruchy, west of Cherbourg.

*Centre Culturel, 4 rue Vastel. Tel: 02 33 23 39 30. Open: May–Sept, daily, standard hours (see pp186–7). Closed: Sun & Mon mornings. Oct–Apr, Tue–Sun, afternoons only. Free admission.*

## Musée de la Libération

The Fort du Roule, 112m (367ft) above Cherbourg, looks out across the *digues* (breakwaters) planned in the 17th century but not completed for 200 years. More 'experience' than museum, since its revamping in 1994, it contrasts the bleakness of the Occupation years with the relief of Liberation. Take the shuttle bus up from the bottom of the hill.

*Tel: 02 33 20 14 12. Open: May–Sept, standard hours (see pp186–7), except Sun & Mon mornings; Oct–Apr, Tue–Sun afternoons. Admission charge.*

Fishing boats on Quai Alexandre III, Cherbourg

# Tour: the Cotentin Coast

Majestic cliffs, empty beaches, 'secret' bays and small, grey-stone villages make this a delightful drive.
*Allow half a day.*

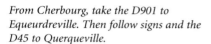

*From Cherbourg, take the D901 to Equeurdreville. Then follow signs and the D45 to Querqueville.*

## 1 Querqueville
St-Germain, the oldest chapel in western France, has survived here for 1,000 years.
*Continue on the D45; at la Rivière, turn left to Château de Nacqueville.*

## 2 Urville-Nacqueville
The English-style gardens and 16th-century great hall of the Château de Nacqueville are open to the public (*see p142*). Before **Landemer** stands the impressively fortified Manoir

du Duc-Écu (private) with a cliff behind, the sea in front. Just past Landemer, a car park on the right tempts visitors to stop and admire the coastal panorama.
*At the entrance to la Quiesce, a tiny right turn leads to Gruchy.*

## 3 Gruchy
White gates, Virginia creeper and roses on the stone cottages reflect the gentrification of this atmospheric seaside village where painter Jean-François Millet was born to a peasant family in 1814.
*Follow signs to Gréville-Hague on the D237.*

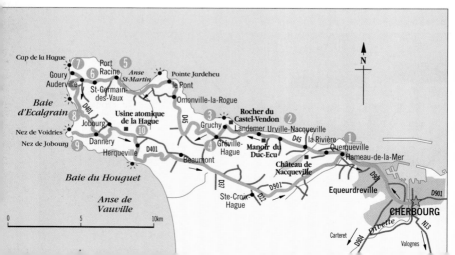

## 4  Gréville-Hague

The stubby 12th-century village church appears in many of Millet's landscapes. His bust faces the main road.

*Turn right on to the D45 to Omonville. After driving along a bramble-hedged lane, the sight of a distant power station comes as a shock. Then the road veers back towards the coast. In Omonville, turn right to Le Pont, a hidden village that looks like a film set. Loop back to the D45; turn right on the coast road which has vast views of Anse St-Martin.*

## 5  Port Racine

At the far end of the bay, punctuated by rocky outcrops in the water, is 'Le Plus Petit Port de France'. Port Racine is minute, just two stone jetties enclosing a dozen rowing boats tied fore and aft.

*Continue on the D45. At the entrance to St-Germain turn right.*

## 6  St Germain-des-Vaux

So quiet is this unspoiled village that roosters strut across the road, confident of being safe from traffic.

*Turn left at the bottom of the hill on to rue Bas; left again at the T-junction on to rue Joignet. Turn right on the D45. At Auderville, turn right to Goury.*

## 7  Goury

The road drops down to Cap de la Hague where the octagonal lifeboat station's two sets of doors enable boats to be launched into the harbour or the open sea, depending on the tides.

*Return to Auderville; turn right on to the D401 (just past a hotel-restaurant).*

## 8  Baie d'Écalgrain

The narrow road affords spectacular views over Goury and even to the Channel Islands on a clear day. Slow down after the hamlet of Écalgrain: the gorse-covered hillside plunges suddenly down to the bay and the dramatic views are distracting.

*In Dannery, turn sharply right to the Nez de Jobourg.*

## 9  Nez de Jobourg

Even on a calm day, the water boils over reefs far below the cliffs of this treeless headland, which is now a bird sanctuary.

*Return to Dannery; rejoin the D401 for Beaumont.*

## 10  Usine Atomique de la Hague

Behind barbed wire, the nuclear power station contrasts with the near-wilderness of the headland. Information is available in summer.

*Return to Cherbourg via Beaumont.*

Stone jetty at Port Racine

## Courseulles-sur-Mer

Courseulles is a small, unsophisticated seaside resort with a broad beach, good oysters and one of the best aquariums in Normandy, **La Maison de la Mer**. After D-Day, its sheltered harbour welcomed Winston Churchill (12 June) and General de Gaulle (14 June). A huge cross of Lorraine (symbol of the free French) marks the spot. Over the River Seulles, however, is Graye, which also has a cross (in the dunes) and also claims the honour of 'de Gaulle's first footsteps back on French soil'.

*On the coast, 18km (11 miles) northeast of Caen, on the D514. La Maison de la Mer: Place General de Gaulle. Tel: 02 31 37 92 58. Open: Feb–Sept, daily, standard hours (see pp186–7); Oct, Nov & Jan, weekend afternoons. Closed: Dec. Admission charge.*

## Coutances

The administrative and religious centre of the Cotentin Peninsula is built on a hill, with the Cathedral of Notre-Dame at the very top. After a fire in 1218, the foundations, towers and nave of the original church were cleverly incorporated into the reconstruction.

The result is notable for its twin spires and 'Le Plomb'. This 40-m (130-ft) high lantern tower illuminates the altar below and was dubbed 'the work of a sublime madman' by 17th-century military engineer, Sébastien Vauban. Join one of the free guided tours (daily in summer, weekends in winter) to fully appreciate what Victor Hugo considered second only to Chartres in beauty.

*75km (47 miles) south of Cherbourg, on the D2.*

## Château Fontaine-Henry

Start with a small fort on the River Mue; build two wings between 1490 and 1550; the result: a lesson in architecture. Looking from right to left, you first see the basic, fortified house, then the 'artistic' middle wing with its three-storey square tower decorated with friezes and pilasters. Finally, there is the extraordinary, wedge-shaped slate roof, steep as a mountain-side. The same family has lived here for five centuries and their collection of paintings and antiques is on view to the public.

*12km (7 1/2 miles) northwest of Caen, off the D22. Tel: 06 89 84 85 57. Open: mid-June–mid-Sept, Wed–Mon,*

Rooftop view over Granville's houses

*afternoons; Easter–mid-June and mid-Sept–Oct, Sat, Sun & bank holiday, afternoons. Admission charge.*

### Gold Beach
The westernmost of the three British sectors on D-Day (*see pp66–9*).

### Granville
Before it became a leisure and pleasure destination in the mid-19th century, the value of this rocky promontory was strategic. Indeed, the military are still based behind the ramparts of the Haute Ville (Upper Town), which withstood a siege in the upheaval after the Revolution. A plaque at the Grand Porte recalls the struggle.

### Musée du Vieux Granville
A collection of costumes and furniture from the region in a historic house.
*2 rue Le Carpentier. Tel: 02 33 50 44 10. Open: daily, except Mon in season. Free admission.*

### Christian Dior Museum
The fashion designer grew up in this elegant clifftop house with its fine gardens. Rotating exhibitions.
*Villa Les Rhumbs, Jardin Public. Tel: 02 33 61 48 21. Open: May–Sept, daily. Admission charge.*

### Îles Chausey
Just 15km (9 miles) offshore, these granite rocks were quarried for Mont-St-Michel and the pavements of Paris and London. The ferocious tide – one of the biggest in the world – rises and falls some 14m (46ft). Grande Île (2km/1¹/₄ miles long) is large enough for a small hotel, a

Château Fontaine-Henry, with the earliest part of the building on the right

fort and a lighthouse. Day trips from Granville take 50 minutes each way to visit the '52 islets and 365 rocks'.

*Granville is on the coast, 105km (65 miles) south of Cherbourg, off the D971.*

### Abbaye d'Hambye
With towering walls but no roof, this ruined 13th-century abbey is imposing yet peaceful, guarded by a steep, wooded escarpment. Though off the beaten track, it is worth the detour up the Sienne Valley for romantics and abbey-enthusiasts. There is also a small library of religious vestments and tapestries. The church and outer buildings can be visited without guides for extended hours.
*3km (2 miles) south of Hambye, on the D51. Tel: 02 33 61 76 92. Open: Apr–mid-Oct, Wed–Mon. Admission charge.*

### Juno Beach
The middle of the three-pronged British attack on D-Day (*see pp66–9*).

# Mont-St-Michel

Some 150m (492ft) above the waves, the gilded statue of the Archangel Michael glistens atop the 100-year-old spire: Mont-St-Michel is a familiar sight from countless postcards and posters. From a distance, the buildings look like outcrops of the rock itself; then the eye picks out half-timbered houses, stone walls, green gardens and the fortress-abbey at the top. A seven-year plan will confine traffic to the mainland and restore the Mount's isolation – eventually.

Buildings have been added and rebuilt on Mont-St-Michel for more than 1,000 years

To avoid the crowds, visit out of season or midweek. Arrive early in the morning or stay the night in one of the 140 hotel rooms so you can wander along cobbled streets in peace. Or, like pilgrims of old, walk from Genêts across the sands with a guide (two hours each way, 12km/ 7$^1$/$_2$ miles in all).

### Maison de la Baie
Here you will get acquainted with the history and natural phenomena of Mont-St-Michel and enjoy an exceptional view over the bay.
*Maison de la Baie du Mont-St-Michel, Rue de la Roche Torin, Cowtils. Tel: 02 33 89 66 00. Open: daily. Admission charge.*

### Porte du Roy (King's Gate)
Two *michelettes* (huge mortars) are reminders of English attacks during the Hundred Years' War. Cross the drawbridge, pass under the portcullis and through the iron gate; to the left is one of the world's best-known restaurants, opened by Mère Poulard a century ago and still serving fluffy omelettes her way, cooked over wood fires. The Grande Rue, just a narrow lane, curves uphill between shops, cafés and restaurants. To avoid the human traffic jams, make for the ramparts and follow the path up to rejoin the main approach to the Grand Degré staircase.

### Mont-St-Michel Abbey and Church
Pity the novice lost in the corridors, chapels and stairways of this enormous complex. From the Terrasse de l'Ouest (Western Terrace), the panorama stretches across to Brittany. Inside the Sacristy, four simple models show how the mount was built: on three levels, with the lower two supporting the top platform with its cloisters, refectory and church, where the present community of three monks and two nuns attend Mass. Over 800 years old, its soaring, barrel-vaulted ceiling is wooden, like that of the cloisters, where a modern picture-window looks straight down to the sea. In the echoing dining room, the windows are cleverly angled to project the voice of the monk reading from the

Bible during meals. Discover your own favourite spots: perhaps the carving of the Bishop of Avranches being 'persuaded' to build the first church (*see pp96–7*), or the huge wooden wheel turned by prisoners' leg-power to haul up supplies from below when this was a gaol after the French Revolution.

Between June and September, *Les Imaginaires*, an intriguing late-night mixture of music and light, brings the ancient buildings to life (*see p152*). *Tel: 02 33 89 80 00. Open: daily. Admission charge.*

### Archéoscope

Here, legends about the Mount are recounted in hi-tech visuals. *Tel: 02 33 89 01 85. Open: Feb–mid-Nov daily, standard hours (see pp186–7). Admission charge (one ticket covers this, the Musée Grévin and Musée Maritime which are open at the same time).*

### Logis Tiphaine

Tapestries and furniture, including a finely carved marriage wardrobe, evoke days gone by. The house was built in 1365 by the Constable of France, Bertrand du Guesclin, and his wife Tiphaine. *Tel: 02 33 60 23 34. Open: daily. Admission charge.*

### Musée Historique

This tells the story of the Mount in dioramas highlighted by light and sound. Children usually demand a look through the periscope. *Tel: 02 33 60 14 09.*

### Musée de la Mer et de l'Ecologie

An explanation of the phenomenon of tides plus 250 models of boats makes this a useful attraction for families. *Tel: 02 33 89 02 02.*

The spire rises through the gentle mist

## Mortain

In the old days this outpost defended southern Normandy from Maine and Brittany; in 1944 it was crucial to Hitler's personally planned counter-attack after the D-Day invasion. In town, the church of St Evroult has an 11th-century doorway decorated with a carved sawtooth pattern. Inside, a 7th-century Anglo-Irish wooden coffer lined with copper bears runic inscriptions; legend maintains that it is the Holy Grail. Indiana Jones has yet to visit!

Largely rebuilt in the 1950s, this hillside town is a good base for exploring the countryside. Two waterfalls, the 24-m (79-ft) Grande Cascade on the River Cance and the Petite Cascade on the River Cançon, are pretty rather than impressive, but make a nice walk on a fine afternoon. Just across the road is the **Abbaye Blanche**, founded in the 12th century. Named after the *dames blanches* (white ladies) of the Cistercian order, it is now occupied by monks.

*63km (39 miles) south of St-Lô, on the D977. Abbaye Blanche. Tel: 02 33 59 00 21. Open: Wed–Mon. Closed: Sun morning (see standard hours, pp186–7). Admission to Abbey is free; charge for art exhibitions in summer.*

## Noron-la-Poterie

Don't be put off by the flowerpots and garden gnomes stacked for sale along the busy D572, southwest of Bayeux. These hide a fine tradition of pottery-making that continues behind the shop-fronts.

*9km (5¹⁄₂ miles) southwest of Bayeux.*

## Port Racine

'France's smallest harbour', a tiny cove on the Cotentin

St-Lo's fortress is a reminder of its war-torn past

### SALT-GLAZE POTTERY

Noron pottery was part of everyday life in the region. Workers took a *bonbonne*, a 5-litre jug of cider, to the fields; the classic *cruchon*, a small jug with handle and stopper, held calvados . . . and still does in many households. The dairy industry used tall, cylindrical *machons* for exporting butter, while coffee is still served in *cannes* (pitchers). The dark brown pottery made from local red clay is sprayed with fine salt during baking to produce a bluish lustre. Random sprinkling gives an attractive irregularity; more salt equals more shine.

Peninsula, is half the size of a football pitch, with a handful of open fishing boats. Two small hotels and a house are the only signs of human habitation on this stretch of the D45 along St Martin's Bay.

*On the coast, 20km (12 miles) northeast of Cherbourg, off the D45.*

## St-Lô

Unsympathetic rebuilding of the 'capital of the ruins' of World War II means St-Lô is bypassed by sightseers. At the church of Notre-Dame, a bare wall fills in the bomb-damaged west front, and on the north side, a shell case remains buried in the stone. The capital of the Manche *département*, the town has a business-like air, but when the French think of St-Lô, they think of horses. The Haras national stud, set up in 1806, has some 200 thoroughbred stallions for breeding trotters, flat race and show-jumping horses.

*65km (40 miles) west of Caen, on the D572. Haras: rue du Maréchal Juin. Tel: 02 33 55 29 09. Open: June–Sept, daily, for guided tours. Special displays: July–Aug on Thur. Telephone for details. Admission charge.*

## St-Vaast-la-Hougue

If the name looks foreign, thank the Scandinavian seafarers who settled around this port, which has seen plenty of action. The English landed here on their way to the Battle of Crécy in 1346, and, in 1692, the combined English and Dutch fleets routed the French navy. Subsequent fortifications give the port character, but today's bustle is due to the 660-berth marina (built in 1982) and a thriving oyster industry (local oysters are supposed to have a 'hint of hazelnut').

*On the coast, 29km (18 miles) southeast of Cherbourg, off the D902.*

## Île de Tatihou

In 1992, to celebrate the tercentenary of the Battle of La Hougue, this island was developed into a leisure park, with nature reserve, restored military fortifications and maritime museum. Boats leave every half hour from St-Vaast.

*Musée Maritime de l'Île Tatihou. Tel: 02 33 23 19 92 for information. Open: Apr–Sept, daily.*

Now a tourist sight, Tatihou's bastions remind visitors of a more turbulent period in history

## Ste-Mère-Église

Fame came to the first commune to be liberated in 1944 when the film *The Longest Day* included scenes of paratrooper John Steele hanging by his parachute from the 13th-century church tower. He hung there for two hours before being rescued by German soldiers.

On the main square, the parachute-shaped **Musée Airborne** is fascinating, with a Douglas C47 and the Horsa glider it towed across the English Channel, crammed with troops of the 82nd and 101st Airborne Division. Glass cases display the trivia of war: occupation bank notes, undetectable German glass mines, shaving cream, first-aid kits and moving letters home. Short films in French and English run continuously.

*Musée Airborne tel: 02 33 41 41 35. Open: Feb–Nov, daily, standard hours (see pp186–7). Admission charge.*

## Ferme-Musée du Cotentin

Imagine the farmhands sitting round the communal table in this 17th-century farmhouse, where cookery demon-strations are popular. Farm and household implements fill the 20 rooms.

*Chemin de Beauvais. Tel: 02 33 95 40 20. Open: Apr–Sept, daily. Admission charge.*

*Ste-Mère-Église is 37km (23 miles) southeast of Cherbourg, on the N13.*

## Utah

The code-name for the western prong of the US attack on D-Day (*see pp66–9*).

## Valognes

The claim to be the 'Versailles of the North' requires a pinch of salt, but this attractive market town does have some grand mansions, including the 18th-century Hôtel de Beaumont, opposite the cider museum. Here, two huge presses are just part of the story of cider-making which goes back some five centuries. The crafts museum, in another old house, features about 20 local crafts in 15 rooms.

## Musée de l'Eau-de-Vie et des Vieux Métiers

A crafts centre-cum-museum with 18 different traditional manual skills

## THE LONGEST DAY (LE JOUR LE PLUS LONG)

The title of Cornelius Ryan's book of D-Day veterans' experiences was also the title of a Hollywood film, with international stars like John Wayne and Robert Mitchum, Curt Jurgens and Arletty. But the phrase was coined by German General Erwin Rommel. On 22 April, 1944, he told his aide-de-camp: 'Believe me . . . the first 24 hours of the invasion will be decisive . . . the fate of Germany will depend on it . . . for the Allies, as well as for us, this will be the longest day.'

on show including Calvados brandy-making.

*Rue Pelouze. Tel: 02 33 40 18 87. Open: Apr–Sept, Wed–Mon; July–Aug, daily. Closed: Sun morning. Admission charge.*

### Musée du Cidre
*Rue du Petit Versailles. Tel: 02 33 40 12 30. Opening hours: as Musée de l'Eau-de-Vie et des Vieux Métiers. Admission charge.*

### Hôtel de Beaumont
*Rue du Versailles Normand. Tel: 02 33 40 12 30. Open: July–mid-Sept, daily, afternoons and Tue morning; also open Easter weekend. Standard hours (see pp186–7). Admission charge.*

*Valognes is 19km (12 miles) southeast of Cherbourg, on the N13.*

### Villedieu-les-Pôeles
True to its name, *poêles* (frying pans) hang in window after window along the main street, the *cuivre* (copper) glinting in the sun. Metal-working here dates back 800 years and continues today. Not only can you hear the hammering of copper but also the clanging of bells in the famous bell foundry, as local craftsmen create everything from casseroles to carillons. A good stop for families, this is a must for food-lovers buying quality cookware.

### Atelier du Cuivre (Copper Workshop)
*54 rue du General-Huard. Tel: 02 33 51 31 85. Open: daily. Closed: Sept–June, Sun. Guided tours available. Free admission.*

### Musée de la Poêlerie et de la Dentellière (Cookware and Lace Museum)
*25 rue du Général-Huard. Tel: 02 33 90 20 92. Open: Easter–mid-Nov, daily; mid-Nov–Easter, standard hours (see pp186–7). Closed: Tue & Sun morning. Admission charge.*

### Musée du Meuble Normand (Museum of Norman Furniture)
*9 rue de Reculé. Tel: 02 33 61 11 78. Open: Easter–mid-Nov, daily; mid-Nov–Easter, standard hours (see pp186–7). Closed: Tue & Sun morning. Admission charge.*

### Fonderie des Cloches (Bell Foundry)
*10 rue du Point Chignon. Tel: 02 33 61 00 56. Open: mid-Feb–Oct, Tue–Sat, standard hours (see pp186–7). Admission charge.*

### Maison de l'Étain (House of Pewter, Tin)
*15 rue du Général-Huard. Tel: 02 33 51 05 08. Open: June–Sept, Mon–Sat, standard hours (see pp186–7). Admission charge.*

*Villedieu-les-Poêles is 77km (48 miles) southwest of Caen, on the N175.*

Suspended in time . . . where parachutist John Steele dangled at Ste-Mère-Église

As the cow symbolises the richness of meadows, so the fishing boat represents the harvest of the Atlantic on the doorstep. The image was captured by 19th-century painters. The reality still chugs in and out of harbours: a raised prow, a stubby mast fore and aft, a blue-smocked sailor in the 'doghouse' on the cramped deck.

Three centuries ago Norman fishermen raided the foggy Newfoundland Banks for cod. These *morutiers* (cod fishermen) salted their catch for markets throughout Europe, and Dieppe, Fécamp and Honfleur grew on the profits. When France lost her Canadian territory, so the Terre-Neuve marine goldmine ran out.

Memories of this heyday of Norman fishing are never far away: museums dedicated to fishermen feature in Dieppe, Granville, Le Havre, Honfleur, and, especially for Terre-Neuve, Fécamp. The annual religious ceremonies for fisherfolk have become festivals for all: Granville in February, Honfleur at Whitsun, or Lieurey, St-Valery-en-Caux, Le Tréport and Dieppe in November, during their herring festivals.

Fewer than 5,000 fishermen plough the seas now, limited by EU regulations and facing competition from Brittany, Cornwall and Ireland. Fresh fish is still sold to locals – on the beach at Étretat, by the harbour in Dieppe and on the quayside in Honfleur. *Criées* (commercial

auctions) send fish off to restaurateurs all over Europe. Before trains linked the coast to Paris, teams of horses would haul the catch, packed in seaweed, to the capital. Today, a chef as far away as the Alps can serve fish that was swimming in the sea 24 hours earlier.

Today's holidaymaker can spend a happy day casting from the beach or renting a boat to venture offshore. There are also freshwater fish in the innumerable small rivers, while chalk streams attract fly-fishermen hopefully stalking trout (*see pp160–61*).

Most towns in Normandy have excellent fish markets, but to make the experience even more pleasurable, try buying on the quayside

# Southern Normandy and Le Mans

Although Normandy's border may have been clearly defined for centuries, there is no dramatic change on leaving the southern *département* of Orne and entering the adjacent areas of non-Norman Mayenne and Sarthe. Mayenne, for example, has cows and half-timbered farmhouses; the local brew is cider.

Beside the Sarthe river in Le Mans

The cathedral and old quarter of Le Mans, capital of Sarthe, would not look out of place in a Norman city. Moreover, the whole region was fought over by the Normans and the rulers of Maine, so most towns still boast at least fragments of fortresses. Domfront, Sillé-le-Guillaume, Lassay-les-Châteaux and Mayenne have imposing ramparts; Ste-Suzanne looks impregnable on its rocky outcrop, while the gatehouse of

Fresnay-sur-Sarthe is a charming museum of women's bonnets.

## Southern Normandy

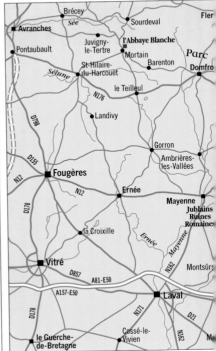

St Julien's Cathedral, from place des Jacobins, Le Mans

Other links include lace-making, centred on Alençon and Argentan, and, above all, the love of horses. Some of the world's finest thoroughbreds, trotters, steeple-chasers and showjumpers are bred here. Neat white railings signal a stud farm, and grandest of all is the **Haras du Pin**, one of the French national studs, with its palatial brick offices and stables. Be there on Thursdays in summer for the musical displays. Across in the Perche region, round Nogent-le-Rotrou, the gentle Percheron horse is king, traditionally used both in battle and farming.

This is a quiet area, with farms and the forests of Sillé and d'Écouves. Bagnoles-de-l'Orne is a spa, complete with lake and clipped lawns; more active holiday-makers take bicycles or canoes to the Alps Mancelles.

Reminders of Roman civilisation include the city wall of Le Mans, a Roman bridge across the river at Beaumont-sur-Sarthe and the ruins of baths at Jublains. Car enthusiasts can have their automobiles blessed at St-Christophe-le-Jajolet or watch the world-famous 24-hour race in Le Mans.

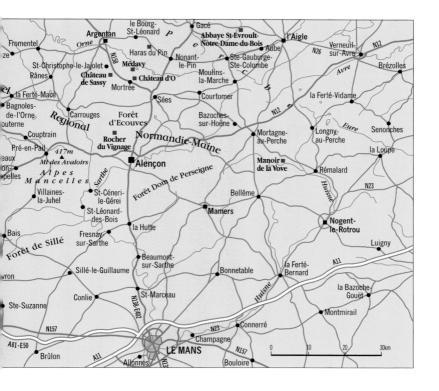

## LE MANS

The annual 24-hour sports car race has made Le Mans world-famous, even if few visit the old city just 3km (2 miles) north of the motor-racing circuit. Although Le Mans is not, and never has been, part of Normandy, its history is inextricably linked with the region. Geoffroy Le Bel, Count of Anjou and Maine, and known as Geoffrey Plantagenet, was born here in 1113. He married Matilda, the granddaughter of William the Conqueror. Their son Henri (born here in 1133) became King Henry II of England, with Normandy and Le Mans part of his realm. Queen Bérengère, widow of King Richard I of England, lived here and founded the Abbaye de l'Épau.

Unusual patterning on the Roman walls which surround the old city

## MEN OF LE MANS

### Automobiles

The Bollée family was important in the development of the automobile. Amédée senior (1844–1917) built a series of steam-driven vehicles. Amédée junior (1867–1926) designed a petrol-engined car in 1896, while Léon (1870–1913) perfected it and applied it to early aeroplanes. Wilbur Wright came from the USA to build and test his biplane at Le Mans.

### Insurance

Le Mans' importance as an insurance centre dates back to Ariste Jacques Trouvé-Chauvel and Jean Marie Lelièvre, who started insurance companies in the 19th century.

### Music

Arnold Dolmetsch (1858–1940) revived interest in early music and in the instruments used to play Renaissance and Baroque compositions. He popularised the recorder in schools.

# Le Mans

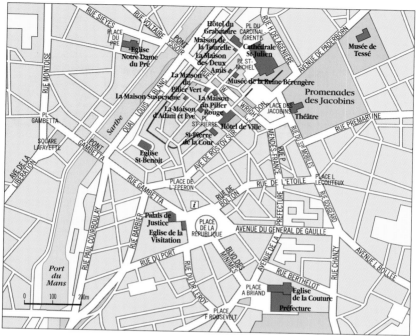

The hill above the River Sarthe was always an ideal position for a fort, and a reminder of early occupation is the menhir, or prehistoric stone, built into the west front of the cathedral. The Romans put a massive wall round what they called Vindunum. That was 1,700 years ago, and some 1,300m (4,265ft) of that enclosure were exposed in the 1980s, though why defences should be embellished with triangles, circles and diamonds of contrasting colours is still a puzzle.

From the 11th century, Le Mans wielded political, economic and religious power and so it naturally became the target of attack for hundreds of years thereafter: by William the

Conqueror in 1063; during the Hundred Years' War with England; and in the Religious Wars of the 16th century. After the French Revolution, the Royalist Vendéens took the city but were in turn crushed in a house-to-house counter-attack. Just as the city was blossoming into prosperity, the Prussians occupied it in 1870. The final devastating blow was given during World War II, when bombs fell after 6,000 Germans were garrisoned there.

The capital of the Sarthe *département*, Le Mans has a population of 150,000 and is known for its thriving insurance businesses and good shopping, including the indoor Centre Jacobins right by the Tourist Office.

## Old Le Mans

The old quarter will look familiar to Gérard Depardieu fans, since much of the film *Cyrano de Bergerac* was shot in the old cobbled streets against a backdrop of half-timbered and stone houses. Details of medieval life remain: keys carved into the pillar at La Maison du Pilier-aux-Clefs (corner Grande Rue and rue St-Honoré) told a largely illiterate population that this was the locksmith's. Much is being restored, but the hustle and bustle is not just from workmen. There are cafés, restaurants and workshops for woodcarvers, jewellers, glass-blowers and artists. Music flows from windows of the Conservatory of Music and Dramatic Art. Since 1986, the first weekend in July brings Les Cénomanies, when locals in costume (and visitors) watch strolling players with lutes, magicians doing tricks, and firework displays. A walk through the ancient lanes (*see pp118–19*) is delightful and proves that Le Vieux Mans is fun without being a theme park of the Middle Ages.

## Cathédrale St-Julien

With no spires topping the towers and a comparatively plain west front, it is bulk, rather than height, that makes this cathedral imposing from the outside. Step inside, however, and the ceilings seem to soar: 24m (79ft) high in the nave, even higher in the transept. Support comes from 54 columns, light from 169 windows.

A fire in 1134 destroyed most of the cathedral, though the side aisles survived. The new nave followed the new style – Gothic. Then in the 13th

Flying buttresses leap from the 13th-century choir of the cathedral

century, the canons decided the Norman choir was too narrow and dark, so the city ramparts were moved to build a 'crown of light'. The chancel and ambulatories rise to 33m (108ft), strengthened by the complex system of flying buttresses which makes the east front so distinctive.

France boasts more stained glass than the rest of the world put together, and St-Julien's is among the oldest examples. The famous Ascension Window (three along from the west door on the south side of the nave) dates from 1140, though with a few modern panes. Note the clarity of the apostles craning their necks heavenwards and the depth of colours. In 1562, during the Religious Wars, the Huguenot zealots destroyed over 50 windows; luckily, many were too high to be reached.

*Place St-Michel, Le Vieux Mans.*
*Open: daily. Free admission.*

## La Maison des Deux Amis

Between Nos 20 and 18 on the rue de la Reine Bérengère, the two friends of the title hold hands. She looks one way, he another. The large wooden shutters of

No 20 would have opened up to form an awning over a shop counter.

### La Maison de la Reine Bérengère

This house was built in 1490, 260 years after the death of Queen Bérengère, so the royal connection is less than tenuous. Carvings here and on the adjacent House of the Annunciation range from the serious (the Virgin and Archangel Gabriel) to the fun (men squashed into tight spaces or being squeezed by a snake). The two houses contain a small museum of regional pottery and paintings.

*9–13 rue de la Reine Bérengère. Tel: 02 43 47 38 80. Open: May–Sept, Tue–Sun, standard hours (see pp186–7); Oct–Apr, Tue–Sun, afternoons. Admission charge.*

### La Maison Suspendue

No prizes for translating the name of this house, with its room overhanging the street. This dates from the 16th and 17th centuries, when the advent of cannon made the medieval walls redundant, so houses were built on and below the ramparts.

*Corner rue de Bouquet and rue St-Pavin de la Cité.*

### Musée de Tessé

The city's art gallery is dedicated to the Tessé family, whose collection was confiscated after the French Revolution. As well as Greek and Egyptian antiquities, there are 14th-century religious works from Siena and paintings by Jacques-Louis David (1748–1825). The main treasure of interest here is the rare 12th-century enamel funeral portrait from the tomb of Geoffroy Le Bel.

*2 ave de Paderborn.*
*Tel: 02 43 47 38 51.*
*Open: Tue–Sun, standard hours (see pp186–7).*
*Admission charge.*

Carving on the tympanum over Cathédrale St-Julien's doorway

# Walk: Old Le Mans

With its half-timbered buildings and narrow lanes, the medieval quarter of Le Mans deserves a whole roll of film. Remember to look up to spot decorative carvings and down for sure footing on the cobbles.

*Allow 45 minutes.*

*Start in the place St-Michel. Pass the cathedral entrance and continue to the northwest corner of the building where a menhir stands at the base. This pagan relic symbolises the old religion, displaced by Christianity.*

## 1  Rue des Chanoines

Immediately on the right is No 27, the Maison de la Tourelle, rich with carvings including a beast's face at the bottom of

the water pipe. It is now the bishop's house, but the cellar was once home to a 'lady of ill repute'.

*Continue along the street. Opposite the wrought-iron gate of No 26 is a tiny statue in a niche: St Sebastian with an arrow piercing his side. Further along, La Maison Saint-Martin houses a jeweller, one of many craftsmen in this area.*

## 2  Square Jacques Dubois

Imagine standing here centuries ago, ready to defend the city. Far below flows the River Sarthe and across lies modern Le Mans. In the 19th century, a tunnel was dug through the hillside to improve access to the city.

*Cross the square with its gardenia trees to two houses facing each other at the start of La Grande Rue.*

## 3  La Grand Rue

On the right is La Maison du Pilier Vert; opposite, La Maison du Pilier Rouge with flecks of red paint still on the pillar. The carved skull and sticks were once thought to denote the house of the executioner, but he lived elsewhere and the sticks were for an annual sporting contest won by the first to hit a ball over the cathedral.

Continue down the street, past the Conservatory of Music and Dramatic Art. Look at the pillar on the corner of rue de l'Écrevisse. The three huge stones prevented carriage wheels damaging the house.

## 4 La Maison d'Adam et Ève

Decide for yourself whether it is Adam and Eve above the doorway or perhaps Bacchus. Look up to see the woman riding a centaur while four musicians provide music. Fish and a man-in-the-moon represent the interests of the original owner, a royal astrologer.

*Continue downhill, noting the keys on the pillar of La Maison du Pilier-aux-Clefs. Look into courtyards, peep through gates. Turn left into the tiny rue Godard and left again into the rue St-Flaceau, built atop the city ramparts. Walk past the cafés in the place St-Pierre, go left on the rue de*

l'Ecrevisse. *At la Grande Rue, return uphill, crossing the square on to the rue de la Reine Bérengère.*

## 5 Rue de la Reine Bérengère

Statues of a man and woman hold hands above the doorways to Nos 18 and 20, where wooden shutters once opened to display the shop's wares. After La Maison des Deux Amis, step through the entrance to the Musée de la Reine Bérengère and into a second courtyard for a dramatic view of the cathedral across the street, admiring more carvings. At the Maison de l'Annonciation, the Virgin awaits the Archangel Gabriel, perhaps amused by the two men with sore necks and five men entwined by a serpent.

*Continue along the street back to the cathedral.*

The ornate red wooden pillar gives this building its name, La Maison du Pilier Rouge

# The 24-hour race

Le Mans and motorsport were linked long before the 24-hour race got under way in 1923. The first ever 'Grand Prix', the Grand Prix de l'Automobile Club de France, was held east of the city in 1906. From the start, wealthy amateurs from all over Europe challenged for honours. After World War II, Jaguars dominated, followed by Ferrari and, in the late 1960s, the Ford GT40. Porsches battled with Matra, Jaguar made a comeback in 1988, and then Mazda of Japan challenged in 1991. The most recent races have been dominated by the German maker Audi, while another revived name from the past – Bentley – has joined Jaguar on the result sheets.

Le Mans can also mean losing and tragedy. In 1952, Pierre Levegh drove single-handed into a four-lap lead only to break down with two hours to go. In 1955, the worst accident in motor racing history occurred: 83 spectators were killed when Levegh's Mercedes hit an Austin-Healey and plunged into the crowd.

## The circuit

The Le Mans start was famous: drivers sprinted across the road, jumped into their cars and zoomed off round the 13.5-km (8-mile) circuit, but this was banned in 1969. Today, after the start, there is a right-hand bend towards the Esses before the even sharper right turn at the Tertre-Rouge. This is the start of the well-known Mulsanne Straight, where drivers accelerate up to 400km/h (249mph). Part of the N138, it is used by ordinary traffic travelling south the rest of the year. At Mulsanne Corner, a virtual hairpin-turn to the right, drivers watch backmarkers, brakes scream and gears crash. The fans love it. Then it's back to the pits and starting line. The whole thing may last only 3½ minutes but it is repeated for 24 hours.

In and around the track, spectators barbecue and drink, brew coffee and eat croissants, go to the funfair in the centre of the track or watch the pit stops. Few stay awake throughout; nowadays, even the cars have crews of three to share the duties.

The 24-hour automobile event is held annually in mid-June.

For information about the 24-hour race, contact **Automobile Club de l'Ouest**: *Circuit des 24 Heures, 72019 Le Mans CEDEX. Tel: 02 43 40 24 24.* You can also visit *www.lemans.org*

Vroom! Speed, skill and burning rubber add up to thrills on the Le Mans circuit

## Nearby
### Abbaye de l'Épau

In the east of Le Mans, near the Lac des Sablons, this abbey was built in 1229 by Queen Bérengère and has been completely restored over the last 30 years. Today, it is best known for its annual Europa Jazz Festival (late April–early May). The queen's tomb still lies in solitary simplicity in the cloisters.
*4km (2¹/2 miles) east of Le Mans. Tel: 02 43 84 22 29.*
*Open: daily, standard hours (see pp186–7). Free admission.*

### Musée de l'Automobile

By the main entrance to the motor-racing circuit, a huge aeroplane-wing-like roof covers the hi-tech Musée de l'Automobile. Among the historic models are the 1896 Tricycle of Léon Bollée and the sleek Porsche that set a circuit record in 1971. There are videos of robots painting cars in modern factories, computer quizzes, and a stomach-churning film of driving through the 'S' bends and into the Mulsanne Straight that 'makes you feel as if you're in the 24-hour race' according to one 10-year-old. Even non-aficionados find this museum interesting, thanks to clips of silly car stunts from silent movies as well as the display, 'Les Costumes des Voyageurs': ladies' elegant silk coats and gentlemen's goggles and gloves from the early days of driving. Trivia nuts can discover interesting facts such as which nation clocks up the most kilometres per year in private cars. The answer, believe it or not, is Finland.
*5km (3 miles) south of Le Mans. Circuit des 24 Heures. Tel: 02 43 72 72 24.*

*Open: daily, standard hours (see pp186–7). Admission charge.*

## Alençon

The capital of the Orne *département* used to be synonymous with fine lace; today, it's a city of plastics, with solid roots in food industries. The rue du Bercail and Grande-Rue are pleasant old streets that intersect outside the 14th-century church of Notre-Dame. Other landmarks include a chapel dedicated to Ste Thérèse, who was born here in 1873. The medieval Ozé House is now the tourist office.

### Musée des Beaux-Arts et de la Dentelle

You can watch a short film in English that explains the town's tradition of lace-making. Compare the handmade lace from Alençon with examples from the rest of the world. Paintings and Cambodian ethnology are also on show.
*12 rue Charles Aveline. Tel: 02 33 32 40 07. Open: daily, standard hours (see pp186–7). Closed: Mon Sept–June. Admission charge.*

*Alençon is 48km (30 miles) north of Le Mans, on the N138.*

### Lace

To counter Venice's monopoly of making fine lace, Alençon was granted the privilege of producing lace for the French court of Louis XIV in 1665. Thanks to the invention of a new, particularly delicate and elegant point (stitch) with tiny bouquets of flowers, Alençon lace was suddenly in demand all over Europe. So jealously guarded was the secret of the pattern that workers only sewed separate sections, so they never knew the complete 'code'. A school of lace maintains the tradition.

## Argentan

A rival to Alençon (45km/28 miles away), Argentan had its own particular lace pattern which was rediscovered by chance in the local archives in 1864. Now the copyright belongs to Benedictine nuns at the local abbey. **La Maison des Dentelles** in the rue de la Noë explains all (*tel: 02 33 87 40 56; open daily*). Somehow, the town's two old churches, St-Germain and St-Nicolas, survived the devastation of the summer of 1944, but most of Argentan has been rebuilt.

*58km (36 miles) southeast of Caen, on the N158.*

## Bagnoles-de-l'Orne

Great claims are made for the springs at this spa town: one legend tells how an old horse called Rapide was the first to benefit, while, according to another, a monk, delighted by his treatment, jumped the 4-m (13-ft) gap between two rocks high above the water. The spot is still known as the Saut du Capucin (Monk's Leap). The Grande Source (Big Spring) jets out water at 25°C (77°F) for body-pummelling showers as well as for drinking. Sufferers from rheumatic and vascular complaints are said to gain most. Neat and tidy, with a lake, racecourse, casino and park, it has obvious attractions for the older generation, but the campsite, 9-hole golf course, and good rock climbing, together with the surrounding forest, make this a peaceful place for holiday-makers, whether or not they take the cure.

*38km (24 miles) southwest of Argentan, off the D916.*

The lake at Bagnoles-de-l'Orne adds to the attractions of this famous spa town

### Beaumont-sur-Sarthe

The tranquil setting belies this town's tempestuous past. William the Conqueror won and lost it three times, and it was fought over by other monarchs. Lumps of the castle walls, demolished in 1617, remain. Don't miss the Roman bridge.

*23km (14 miles) south of Alençon, on the N138.*

### Prieuré de Vivoin

Two kilometres (1 mile) to the east, the handsome 13th-century priory and church with its Hall of Pillars is a tribute to volunteers who restored the ravages of time and the French Revolution. In summer, there are evening concerts.

*Tel: 02 43 97 04 36. Open: Mar–Nov, daily, afternoons. Admission charge.*

### Château de Carrouges

King Louis XI slept here. . . back in August 1473. His hosts, the Le Veneur family, had already been here for a century. They left in 1936 but this red-brick, rectangular castle is still impressive, protected by deep moats and with a fairy-tale gatehouse with steep slate roofs. In the grounds are a craft centre as well as the visitors' centre for the Normandy-Maine Regional Nature Park, spread out below the château.

*29km (18 miles) northwest of Alençon, on the D909. Tel: 02 33 27 20 32.*
*Open: daily, standard hours (see pp186–7).*
*Admission charge.*

One of the fine state rooms at Château de Carrouges

## Domfront

On a clear day, the view from the fortress over the Passais region stretches to Mont Marganfin, some 13km (8 miles) to the south. When England's King Henry II and his love, Eleanor of Aquitaine, held court here in the 12th century, this was a fearsome stronghold. Now only a few thick walls in the public gardens remain, though from rue des Fossés-Plisson you can still see where towers jutted up from the medieval ramparts. The narrow rue du Docteur-Barrabé still has half-timbered houses and Notre-Dame-sur-l'Eau has had some of its 12th-century beauty restored, including the frescoes. Damage here was not from the war but from 19th-century road builders.

*36km (22 miles) north of Mayenne, on the D962.*

## Évron

Every year, on the first weekend in September, the Festival de la Viande (Festival of Meat) features some of the finest flesh in France to the delight of the chefs' Confrérie de l'Entrecôte (Brotherhood of Steak). The rest of the year, the Gothic basilica is the draw for pilgrims who pray at the 13th-century, silver-covered, carved wooden figure of Notre-Dame de l'Épine (Our Lady of the Thorn).

*57km (35 miles) northwest of Le Mans, off the A81.*

## La Ferté-Macé

If Évron is all about beef, this town is all about tripe, prepared *en brochette*, using gras-double, three of the four stomachs of the cow, wrapped round pieces of cow foot and cooked on a kebab-like wooden skewer. Eat them as locals do at the Thursday-morning open-air market.

*46km (29 miles) northwest of Alençon, on the D916.*

## Fresnay-sur-Sarthe

The main town of the Alpes Mancelles, Fresnay has a medieval quarter with cobbled streets, ancient houses and the remains of defences against Normandy. The postern-gate with its twin towers now houses the **Musée des Coiffes**, devoted to headwear. Through the gate, a garden leads to sheer walls above the River Sarthe. The town makes a good base for exploring the quiet Sarthe Valley and the forest of Sillé.

*Musée des Coiffes. Tel: 02 43 97 22 20. Open: Mar–June & Sept, Sun & holidays, daily; July–Aug, daily. Admission charge.*

*Fresnay-sur-Sarthe is 20km (12 miles) southwest of Alençon, off the N138.*

## Jublains Ruines Romaines

These Roman ruins are in the middle of nowhere; fields stretch in all directions, and Mayenne is some 10km (6 miles) away. Excavations are slowly revealing more clues to this square Roman fort. An audiovisual display in the recently renovated archaeological museum explains how the hot and cold baths (which can be clearly seen) used to work. Parts of the ruins can be wandered freely.

*14km (9 miles) northwest of Évron, on the D7. Tel: 02 43 04 30 16. Call in advance to ensure the museum will be open. Closed: Feb. Admission charge.*

## Lassay-les-Châteaux

Marked 'Lassay' on most maps, the full name refers to the three castles in the immediate area. Without being unkind to the châteaux of Bois-Thibault and Bois-Frou, it is the fortress in Lassay itself that attracts military historians as well as children. For over 500 years, its drawbridge, barbican, ramparts and eight stubby, circular towers have dominated the surrounding countryside.

*16km (10 miles) southwest of Bagnoles-de-l'Orne, on the D34. Tel: 02 43 04 74 33. Open: Easter–May, Sat & Sun; June–Sept, daily. Admission charge.*

## Laval

Outside the old walls, the *préfecture* (capital) of the Mayenne *département* is a modern city; within are twisting streets with half-timbered houses clustering around what is left of the old castle. Here, the museum honours favourite son **Henri Rousseau**, the 19th-century painter nicknamed 'Le Douanier', with a large international collection of Naïve Art. Although displaying only one of his paintings, it does have his reconstructed studio, complete with paint box and easel. Rousseau was born in the south tower of the Porte Beucheresse, the old city gate which still stands. His grave in La Perrine Park bears a moving inscription, carved as if handwritten, by the poet Apollinaire, an admirer of his work.

From the 16th to 18th centuries, Laval was an important textile-producing town, and mansions such as the Maison du Grand Veneur (Master of the Royal Hunt's House) at the corner of the Grand Rue and rue des Orfèvres attest to its prosperity. Another is the Maison de Clermont at No 8 rue de la Trinité, where six statuettes parade across the façade. Today it is home to France's largest dairy conglomerate.

## Lactopôle

A glitzy visit to the glories of dairy products, and a fascinating reminder of the manual past and industrial future of this delicious foodstuff.

*Tel: 02 43 59 51 90. Open: July–Aug, Mon–Fri, and by appointment all year. English-speaking guides available. Admission charge.*

## Bateau-Lavoir 'Le Saint-Julien'

This floating laundry, with big copper kettles, dating to the late 19th century was in use until 1970!

*Tel: 02 43 53 39 89. Open: July–Aug, Tue–Sun. Admission charge.*

## Musée du Vieux Château

*Tel: 02 43 53 39 89. Open: Tue–Sun, standard hours (see pp186–7). Admission charge.*

*Laval is 83km (52 miles) west of Le Mans, off the A81.*

## Mayenne

Although in the *département* of Mayenne and astride the River Mayenne, this small, quiet town is best known as the starting and finishing point for boating holidays.

The crumbling fortress on the west bank is undergoing a massive face-lift which will last several years. Mansions on the place Cheverus and place de Hercé may be admired from the outside only since they are private. This is a place for strolling rather than for staying.

*88km (55 miles) northwest of Le Mans, via the A81, N162.*

Autumn in Mortagne-au-Perche

## Mortagne-au-Perche

Weekends bring Parisians to this hilly and misty region that gave its name to the sturdy Percheron horses bred from Saracen stallions abandoned by the Moors in the 8th century. Mortagne itself is famous for *boudin* (*see box*) and kilometres of it are sold during the annual Black Pudding Fair midway through Lent. In the flamboyant Gothic church of Notre-Dame, a stained-glass window commemorates locals who moved away to settle in Canada in the 17th century.

## Maison des Comtes du Perche/Musée Alain

'I am a Percheron, that's to say, different from a Norman,' said Emile Chartier. The museum pays tribute to this philosopher, known simply as 'Alain', who was born here in 1868.
*8 rue du Portail-St-Denis. Tel: 02 33 25 25 87. Open: Tue–Sat, afternoons. Free admission.*

*Mortagne-au-Perche is 38km (24 miles) east of Alençon, off the N12.*

## Nogent-le-Rotrou

During the French Revolution, many symbols of the aristocracy were destroyed, so it is a tribute to the Duc de Sully (who died in 1641) that his tomb in the Hôtel-Dieu remained unharmed. King Henri IV's chief minister was admired for his support for French farmers, declaring that the 'real gold mines of France were her *bourage* (ploughing) and *pastourage* (meadows)'.

In the ruined castle, the **Musée Saint Jean** records local life and artisanal crafts, from glass to iron. *Tel: 02 37 52 18 02. Open: Wed–Mon, standard hours.*

*Nogent-le-Rotrou is 74km (46 miles) northeast of Le Mans, on the N23.*

## Château d'O

As romantic as any château of the Loire Valley, this has a fairy-tale quality, with its steep roofs and enclosing moat. Its three wings embody three periods of architecture: the 15th century (east wing), 16th century (south wing), and 18th century (west wing). Despite the brevity of the surname, the O family was, for four generations, one of the most powerful in France, from Jean d'O, a counsellor to King

### BOUDIN

Mortagne's gift to French rural cuisine, *boudin* (black pudding), is a gourmet speciality made from pigs' blood and coiled like a black rubber hose. With forests full of wild pigs, the Percheron peasants had ample opportunity to develop their skills in *charcuterie*. To preserve this heritage, the Confrèrie des Chevaliers du Goûte-Boudin (the Knights of the Black Pudding Brotherhood) invented a Black Pudding Fair in 1963. Surprise! – entries from England and Scotland scooped some of the top prizes.

Charles VII at the end of the 15th century, to François d'O, finance minister a century later to both King Henri III and King Henri IV. Renovations inside have recently revealed *trompe-l'oeil* paintings. The Salon des Muses is painted with life-like statues of goddesses, while in the adjacent gallery visitors crane their necks to admire swooping eagles.
*Near Mortrée, 15km (9 miles) southeast of Argentan. Tel: 02 33 35 34 69. Open: Wed–Mon, afternoons.*

### Haras du Pin

Jules Hardouin-Mansart, 17th-century architect, who remodelled Versailles, also designed this 'Versailles of the Horse'. Away from main roads, on the edge of an oak forest, France's most famous national stud is a pink-brick mansion and stables enclosing a courtyard of lawn and gravel paths. Residents include some of the world's finest stallions: thoroughbreds for racing and trotting, saddlehorses for show-jumping and Anglo-Arabs for steeplechasing. Even the ancient Percheron breed has been preserved. But the Haras does more than produce champions; it trains people, from grooms to breeders, to continue the traditions of France's 22 studs.

A brisk guided tour is available all year round, but even better are the *musicales du jeudi*, the Thursday afternoon practice sessions conducted to music in summer. Guided tours are given every half-hour.
*12km (7¹/₂ miles) east of Argentan, on the N26. Tel: 02 33 36 68 68. Open: daily. Closed: Oct–Mar, mornings. Admission charge.*

Fittingly splendid gateway to the national stud of Haras du Pin

### St-Cénéri-le-Gérei

No wonder this hamlet is crowded with visitors in the height of summer: its title of 'one of the most beautiful villages in France' is fully justified. Cottages sit on a small rocky outcrop above the burbling River Sarthe, while the small church with its saddleback roof at the top of the village has bold 13th-century frescoes in the choir. The artist Corot came here over a century ago and today there are still artists' studios where the painters and potters who live here all year round show off their wares.

*53km (33 miles) northwest of Le Mans, on the D101.*

### St-Christophe-le-Jajolet

If you want to have your car blessed, be here the last Sunday in July or the first Sunday in October and join the procession of cars past the church dedicated to St Christopher, patron saint of travellers. Inside the church, note the delightful mural of a 1920s' goggled driver and pilot.

*8km (5 miles) south of Argentan, off the N158.*

### Château de Sassy

The building of this mansion was interrupted by the Revolution: no doubt the owner, the lawyer of King Louis XVI, was attending his client in prison. The monarch lost his head but a lock of his hair is here, along with a legal library amassed by the Pasquier family over the centuries. The classic formal gardens are famous (*see p142*).

*Tel: (02) 33 35 32 66.*
*Gardens open: daily.*
*Free admission.*

The quiet interior of Maison Fouquet at Ste-Suzanne

*Château open: Palm Sun–Oct, daily, afternoons.*
*Admission charge.*

### St-Léonard-des-Bois

In the heart of the Alpes Mancelles, the River Sarthe loops past the Grand Fourché, a towering, wooded escarpment, then rounds a meadow, which in summer is a busy campsite. This hamlet of stone houses makes a good base for hiking well-marked trails. Despite its name, the Vallée de Misère (the Vale of Tears) provides an enjoyable morning walk past the Manoir de Linthe and through unspoilt countryside.

*49km (30 miles) northwest of Le Mans, on the D258.*

### Ste-Suzanne

Not many fortresses got the better of William the Conqueror, but after a four-year siege here, he finally gave up. The triangular outcrop of rock 70m (230ft) above the River Erve was taken by the English during the Hundred Years' War, but the French won it back 15 years later, thanks to the help of an Englishman married to a local girl. Saint Suzanne is the patron saint of the betrothed. Today, shops and art galleries huddle below the castle's huge walls which protect a church and restored buildings, including the **Musée de l'Auditoire** (Audience Chamber Museum), whose display of weights and measures through the ages ranges from shoe sizers to opium scales. Built into the ramparts is the elegant yet plain 17th-century country house of Fouquet de la Varenne, founder of the French postal service.

*50km (31 miles) west of Le Mans, off the A81, on the D7. Musée de l'Auditoire tel: 02 43 01 42 65. Open: Mar–Oct, daily, afternoons. Admission charge.*

### Sées

British tourists often stop here after a ferry crossing to Caen, perhaps attracted by the red telephone box across from the 13th-century cathedral. Beneath the two spires resembling inverted ice-cream cones is a clear, uncluttered nave with no side chapels. A tape-recorded history, backed with organ music, leaps into life at the touch of a button: the acoustics are superb.

*22km (14 miles) north of Alençon, on the N138.*

### Sillé-le-Guillaume

Spilling down a very steep hillside, Sillé is dominated by a massive 15th-century castle that looks even more menacing than William the Conqueror's original fortress. Built to protect Maine from the Normans, the keep stands 40m (131ft) high, complete with machicolations. Nowadays, however, the nearby lake and forest of Sillé draw visitors for sailing, cycling and walking. *32km (20 miles) northwest of Le Mans, on the D304.*

Detail from the mural in the church of St-Christophe-le-Jajolet

# By bike: the Alpes Mancelles

The 'alps of Le Mans' recently celebrated their centenary as a recognised tourist attraction. These tumbling hills are on the southern fringe of Normandy. This quiet, scenic route is only 24km (15 miles), but is a stern test for gears and thighs.

*Take the N12 west from Alençon; follow signs to the Alpes Mancelles and begin the route at St-Pierre-des-Nids.*

## 1  St-Pierre-des-Nids

Many cyclists stay in M. Etienne's *auberge*, Le Dauphin, directly opposite the church. Thanks to a local campaign, the bells are silent at night . . . to the benefit of tourists and locals alike.
*Leave the village on the D144 towards St-Cénéri-le-Gérei.*

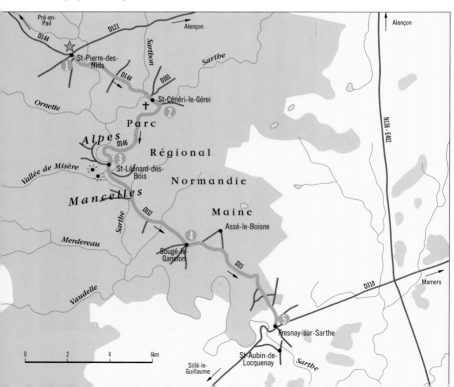

## 2 St-Cénéri-le-Gérei

After a roller-coaster ride through fields and farms, the road leads up to St-Cénéri. Perched on a hill, this artists' colony of carefully restored stone cottages revels in the designation 'one of the prettiest villages in France'. Not only the art galleries but also some of the studios are open to the public; watch an artist or craftsman at work, then pause at a café before climbing up to the simple 12th-century church with its old frescoes, tombs built into the walls and vistas over the valleys. (*See also p130.*)
*Take the D146 to St-Léonard-des-Bois. After a short, steep descent out of St-Cénéri, the road crosses the River Sarthe; glance right for a view of the church, with the cliff dropping away below. Then continue through open fields and thick chestnut woods, past high hedges and farms selling goat cheese.*

## 3 St-Léonard-des-Bois

Four steep hills overlook the River Sarthe as it curves past this village. Thick woods give way to open water meadows; the bridge is adorned with flower boxes, and collectors of churches can add another 12th-century one to their list. The small population swells in summer, thanks to the campsite, and there are several places for refreshment or for purchasing the makings of a picnic. (*See also p130.*)

Clear and simple signage

*Continue on the D112 to Sougé-le-Ganelon. As the road flattens, look right for the Manoir de Linthe. Dating from the 11th century, the round tower was originally a dovecote. Follow the River Sarthe, watching for fishermen in waders casting for trout.*

## 4 Sougé-le-Ganelon

The horizon is broken by the spire of the hilltop church. Apricot-coloured houses on the edge of the village contrast with the covered public wash house, complete with pump, halfway up to the main square.
*Follow signs in the village to the D15 and Fresnay. The road follows the ridge of hills, with the river glittering below.*

## 5 Fresnay-sur-Sarthe

Locals claim their church resembles Mont-St-Michel . . . from a distance. Behind it is the ancient heart of town, with narrow, cobbled streets and small shops. The old market hall in the place Thiers has been preserved and cleverly glassed in. A sculpture-cum-fountain of a lion and a tree represents the town's coat of arms. The open place de la Mairie leads to twin towers housing a museum of headwear (*see p126*). Beyond is a public garden and the ruins of battlements above the sheer drop to the river.
*The route ends here. There are cafés and hotels for refreshment or to stay the night.*

# King Harold's revenge

The English have long been regular visitors to Normandy. Many drive through to points farther south, others settle in for holidays. In the past ten years, however, a new breed has emerged: the property owner. With the abolition of currency exchange controls and the freedom of movement permitted within the European Union, cross-border house purchases became straightforward. So, when property prices in southern England sky-rocketed in the 1980s, English families searching for second homes looked to Normandy, where prices seemed a bargain.

The younger generation of Normans were leaving the land to live in towns; the older generation wanted comfortable modern villas; neither wanted to keep up the old family home in the country. The English, however, are passionate about 'doing up' houses . . . the older the better. Although there has been some resentment, relations are generally good; often a neighbouring farmer keeps an eye on the house in exchange for using a field or collecting apples from the orchard. The English come for holidays and lend their *résidences secondaires* (second homes) to family and friends; some have become permanent residents, joining in the life of the local community.

Purchasing a house is simple. Some French *agences immobilières* (estate agents) specialise in overseas sales. The local *notaire* (notary) oversees the *sous-seing privé* (private agreement) between

SIGRID
OF CHELSEA
LONDON

buyer and seller that is both more binding and expedited more smoothly than the English equivalent.

The English on their overcrowded island are also lured by recreation facilities. New golf courses have been carved out of the lush pastureland; queues are unknown. While 'full' signs may be common in England's south coast marinas, Normandy has built some 20 *ports de plaisance* with 10,000 berths to attract British sailors. With the recession, the impetus has lessened but the tide has not turned.

Signs of the times – the foreign invasion of France: boat names clearly spell out ownership (facing page); estate agents (below) thrive on business from abroad

# Getting away from it all

*'The view is superb, the sea always the sea! . . .*
*This sea is something totally different from the*
*Mediterranean, at one and the same*
*time mean and great.'*

ÉMILE ZOLA
*Zest for Life*, 1875

Sunshine, blue skies and
the soul of restfulness

## BEACHES

Normandy's beaches have attracted sea-bathers for nearly two centuries. Sadly, the heavy traffic in the English Channel has led to heavy pollution all along the coasts on both sides of the water. The French government carries out tests in accordance with European Union regulations and grades the quality of the beaches.

Category A beaches have 'good-quality water conforming with EU directives'. All but one of these are in the Manche *département*.

Beaches are listed by nearest town/village and location.

### In Manche

From the southeast, going anticlockwise round the peninsula, these are the best beaches. Many are opposite or at the end of small roads that lead to the sea.

**Ste-Marie-du-Mont**
Utah Beach.
**St-Martin-de-Varreville**
By the Monument Leclerc.
**St-Germain-de-Varreville**
Opposite D129 road.
**St-Marcouf-de-l'Isle**
Les Gougins beach.
**St-Vaast-la-Hougue**
La Hougue beach.
**Barfleur**
La Sambière beach.
**Gouberville**
Le Bas de la Rue.
**Néville**
Opposite D514 road.
**Réthoville**
Opposite D226 road.
**Cosqueville**
Le Vicq beach.
**Fermanville**
Anse de la Mondrée bay, Bretteville en Sarthe beach.
**Querqueville**
By the Camping des

Armées campsite.
**Les Pieux**
Sciotot beach.
**Le Rozel**
Opposite campsite.
**Surtainville**
Opposite D66 road.
**Beaubigny**
Opposite D131 road.
**Barneville-Carteret**
North side of the promontory.
**St-Jean-de-la-Rivière**
Opposite D166.
**Portbail**
Opposite CRS post.
**St-Lô-d'Ourville**
Lindbergh-Plage beach.
**St-Rémy-des-Landes**
Opposite D327 road.
**Surville**
Opposite D526 road.
**Glatigny**
Opposite D337 road.
**Bretteville-sur-Ay**
Opposite D136 road.
**Pirou**
Opposite D94 road.
**Agon-Coutainville**
Central beach.

**Annoville**
Opposite D537 road.
**Lingreville**
Opposite D220 road.
**Bréhal**
Opposite D592 road.
**Coudeville**
Opposite D351 road.
**Granville**
Le Plat Gousset beach.
**Jullouville**
Les Sapins beach, Carolles beach.
**Champeaux**
Sol Roc beach.

**In Seine-Maritime**
**Veulettes-sur-Mer**
Veulettes beach.

**European Blue Flag Award winners**
Ten beaches in Normandy hold the highest honour:
• Dieppe (Dieppe Plage)
• Veules-les-Roses
• Merville Francville Plage
• Ouistreham
• Courseulles-sur-Mer
• Néville-sur-Mer
• Barneville-Carteret
• St-Georges-de-la-Rivière
• Bréhal
• Bréville-sur-Mer.

**LAKES AND INLAND WATERS**
The same controls govern the quality of inland water facilities with the same categories awarded, from A to D (pass to fail). The cleanest of these are:
**Calvados**
Pont-l'Évêque
Plan d'eau de Pont-l'Évêque.
**Orne**
La Ferté.
Brochardière.
**Eure**
Poses.
Base Plein Air et Loisirs-Zone Verte.
**Manche**
Le Val-St-Père at le Gué-de-l'Épine.

Joyous colours at the beach

## NATURAL PARKS
Normandy has four regional parks:
Parc Naturel Régional de Brotonne,
Marais du Cotentin et du Bessin, Parc
Naturel Régional de Normandie-Maine
and Parc Natural Regional de Perche,
all extending into several thousands of
hectares with a host of flora and fauna.

### Parc Naturel Régional de Brotonne
The park's heart is the Forêt de
Brotonne itself, a vast beech forest
south of Caudebec-en-Caux. The
protected area, however, is much larger,
a total of 58,000 hectares. On the south
bank of the Seine, pretty drives include
the Route des Chaumières (Thatched
Cottage Trail), between La Mailleraye-
sur-Seine and the Vernier Marshes.
A dozen small 'eco-museums' feature
the traditions of the Brotonne.

### Maison du Parc (Park Service HQ)
*76940 Notre-Dame-de-Bliquetuit,*
*southeast of the Pont-de-Brotonne.*
*Tel: 02 35 37 23 16. Open: Apr–Oct,*
*daily; Nov–Mar, Mon–Fri.*

### Maison de la Pomme (Apple Museum)
This museum examines the role of the
apple in Norman life.
*Ste-Opportune-la-Mare. Tel: 02 32 57*
*16 48. Open: contact for details.*
*Admission charge.*

### The Forge
The original village blacksmiths.
*Ste-Opportune-la-Mare.*
*Tel: 02 32 57 16 48. Open: Mar, Apr, Nov,*
*Dec, 1st Sunday of month, afternoon;*
*July–Aug, Sat & Sun, afternoons.*
*Admission charge.*

### Maison du Lin (Flax Museum)
Everything you ever wanted to know
about flax for making linen. Upper
Normandy is one of Europe's leading
producers of flax.
*Routot. Tel: 02 32 56 21 76.*
*Open: Apr–Sept, Wed–Mon, afternoons;*
*July–Aug, daily, afternoons.*
*Admission charge.*

### Maison des Métiers (Crafts Museum and Workshops)
On Sundays craftsmen demonstrate
their skills at this centre of traditional
farming techniques.
*Bourneville. Tel: 02 32 57 40 41.*
*Open: Mar–Nov, Sat & Sun; May–Oct,*
*Wed–Mon; July–Aug, daily. Admission*
*charge for museum.*

### Four à Pain (Bread Oven)
Claude Dambry makes crusty loaves the
old-fashioned way every Sunday from
March to November in this museum of
country baking.
*La Haye-de-Routot. Tel: 02 32 57 07 99.*
*Open: Mar–Nov, Sun, afternoons; July–*
*Aug, daily, afternoons. Admission charge.*

### Musée du Sabotier (Clogmakers' Museum)
France's only collection of *sabots*
(clogs) from this region and from
the neighbouring countries is
on show.
*La Haye-de-Routot. Tel: 02 32 57 59 67.*
*Open: as Four à Pain. One admission*
*ticket covers both attractions.*

### Le Monde Merveilleux des Abeilles (The Wonderful World of Bees)
You can observe the life of busy honey

Beech glades (above) in Perseigne Forest, east of Alençon, a haven of peace and quiet (top)

bees through the special window of their beehive.
*Mesnil-sous-Jumièges, Le Halage. Tel: 02 35 91 36 76. Open: Apr–Oct, daily, afternoons. Admission charge.*

### Moulin à Vent (Windmill)
Given enough wind, this restored stone windmill grinds flour as it did in the 13th century. The former Miller's House reflects the importance of this traditional form of energy.
*Hauville. Tel: 02 32 56 57 32. Open: Apr–Sept, Sun, afternoons; July–Aug, daily, afternoons.*

### Marais du Cotentin et du Bessin
Local villages have combined to preserve 120,000 hectares (296,526 acres) of this important breeding ground for flora and fauna. The marshes, rich grazing ground in spring and summer, usually flood in autumn and winter, so dikes and elevated roads are a feature. The 25,000 hectares (61,776 acres) of marshes surrounding Carentan are on the eastern side of the Cotentin 'neck', where rivers like the Douve and Taute flow to the sea. On the migration route between Northern Europe and Africa, these marshes are a paradise for birdwatchers. There are boat trips along the canals and rivers, even horse-drawn caravan rides in summer.
*Maison du Parc Cantepie, BP282, 50500 Les Veys. Tel: 02 33 71 65 30.*

### Parc Naturel Régional de Normandie-Maine
Like Brotonne, this 234,000-hectare (578,227-acre) area embraces heritage as well as nature. There are 45,000 hectares (111,197 acres) of mainly beech forest such as Andaine, Écouves, Mortain, Perseigne and Sillé, as well as classic small, hedged fields of the *bocage*. Add in the rocky outcrops and gorges, lakes and rivers, and this is a peaceful, if popular, place for lovers of the outdoors.

### Maison du Parc
Full details of all the activities available can be had from the park headquarters in Carrouges.
*BP05, 61320 Carrouges. Tel: 02 33 81 75 75.*

**Canoeing:** on the Sarthe, Mayenne and Varenne rivers.

**Cycling, riding and walking:** on marked trails through the park.

**Rock climbing:** in Andaine forest there are rock faces specially designated for climbers; in Mortain, the Aiguille (needle) and the Fosse-Arthour gully are well-known challenges for climbers.

### Parc Naturel Régional de Perche
In the heart of the former province of the Perche, the Nature Park was established in 1998, extending across the area between the plains of Beauce and the Normandy *bocage*. The park covers 182,000 hectares (449,732 acres) and contains a broad spectrum of plant and animal life. Full details can be obtained from the park service headquarters at Nocé.
*Maison du Parc Courboyer BP15, 61340 Nocé. Tel: 02 33 25 70 10.*

### GARDENS
The Normans are keen gardeners. Cottages have tidy plots of vegetables and

flowers; châteaux, of course, have specially designed terraces, beds and parks. Some of these show the influence of English neighbours across the Channel, others look to Italy and Holland; most, however, are in the great French tradition of horticulturalists such as André Le Nôtre.

### Beaumesnil

Château de Beaumesnil boasts a 350-year-old garden designed by Le Nôtre's contemporary, Jean de la Quintinie. As well as the classic formal garden there is a box tree maze on a ruined keep and a mirror lake (*see p71*).
*Tel: 02 32 44 40 09. Open: Apr–Sept, daily (except Tue). Closed: Tue. Admission charge.*

### Beaumont-Hague

The Château de Vauville garden could be on the Côte d'Azur rather than the English Channel, thanks to its collection of bamboo and yucca, agave and aloe.

*Tel: 02 33 52 71 41. Open: July–Aug, daily, afternoons; May–June, Tue, Fri, Sat, Sun, afternoons; Sept, Tue, Sat, Sun, afternoons. Admission charge.*

### Caen

The 250-year-old Jardin des Plantes is the city's pride and joy, along with the Vallée des Jardins nearby. It's worth checking out the guided tours that take place on some Saturday afternoons.
*5 place Blot. Tel: 02 31 30 48 30. Open: daily. Free admission.*

### Giverny

Claude Monet Gardens (*see p48*).

### Martinvast

The Parc de Martinvast has 175-year-old gardens laid out in the English style.
*Tel: 02 33 87 20 80. Open: year round. Closed: Sat, Sun and bank holiday mornings; Nov–Mar, Sat all day. Admission charge.*

The bridge and water lilies at Giverny – Monet's inspiration

## Mézidon-Canon

The De Mézerac family have toiled long and hard to make the Château de Canon garden into one of Normandy's gems. It has a scarlet Chinese pavilion and a ruined castle, a reflecting pool and the Chartreuses walled gardens.
*Tel: 02 31 20 05 07. Open: June–Sept, Sat & Sun, afternoons.*
*Admission charge.*

## Offranville

Visitors who pay homage to the writer Guy de Maupassant at the Château de Miromesnil can also enjoy an authentic Victorian-style kitchen garden with vegetables and flowers carefully interspersed (*see p51*).
*Tel: 02 35 85 02 80. Open: Apr–Oct, daily, afternoons. Admission charge.*

## St-Christophe-le-Jajolet

The Château de Sassy typifies the formal French garden, where nature conforms to order. Box hedges are clipped, even trees are controlled.
*Tel: 02 33 35 32 66. Open: Easter–Oct, daily, 3–6pm. Admission charge.*

## Thury-Harcourt

The Parc et Jardins du Château d'Harcourt occupies three levels of a 70-hectare site in the beautiful Suisse Normande.
*Tel: 02 31 79 72 05. Open: Mar–mid-June & mid-Sept–mid Nov, Wed–Mon, afternoons; mid-June–mid-Sept, daily, 10.30am–6.30pm. Admission charge.*

## Urville-Nacqueville

West of Cherbourg, the Château de Nacqueville boasts an English garden in a sheltered valley. Azaleas and rhododendrons surround the lake; lilies border a tinkling stream.
*Tel: 02 33 03 21 12. Open: Easter–Sept, Wed, Thu & Sat–Mon, afternoons. Admission charge.*

## Varengeville-sur-Mer

The Parc Floral des Moutiers on the Dieppe cliffs was designed by the influential landscape gardener Gertrude Jekyll. The magnolias are outstanding.
*8km (5 miles) west of Dieppe. Tel: 02 35 85 10 02. Open: mid-Mar–mid-Nov, daily, standard hours. Admission charge.*

## FORESTS

'Cathedral-like' is an over-used cliché to describe forests but in Normandy it is actually true. Standing tall and straight, the *hêtres* (beech) could be the columns of a nave, their spreading leaves the roof. Some woods are small, for example by the abbey around Cérisy-la-Forêt, but there are half-a-dozen over 5,000 hectares (12,355 acres), all with roads for cars and paths for walking.

## Seine-Maritime

In northeastern Normandy there are over 9,000 hectares (22,239 acres) of beech trees: the *haute* (upper) and *basse* (lower) forests of Eu, separated by the villages of Fallencourt and Foucarmont. The middle of the *département*, inland from Dieppe, boasts the forest of Eawy. Use the small town of St-Saëns as a base to explore the 6,500 hectares (16,062 acres) of timberland. Straddling the border with Eure is Normandy's largest and, arguably, France's best beech forest: the Forêt de Lyons (11,000 hectares/27,182 acres).

Some 9km (5½ miles) north, on the N31, is the Hêtre de la Bunodière, an ancient 40-m (131-foot) tall tree.

**Eure**

A mixture of beech, pine and oak, the Brotonne Forest is in the Parc Naturel Regional de Brotonne (*see p138*).

**Orne**

The forest of Andaine, part of the Normandy-Maine Regional Nature Park,

is between Bagnoles-de-l'Orne and Juvigny. The fit can admire the 5,300 hectares (13,097 acres) from the top of the observation tower of Bonvouloir on the D235. There is another tower in the middle of the forest of Écouves, north of Alençon: 8,000 hectares (19,768 acres) of mixed woodland, full of deer.

**Sarthe**

East of Alençon is the Perseigne Forest, full of beech glades.

A typical Normandy beech forest; this is Perseigne, Vallée d'Enfer

# Shopping

As in the rest of France, food is top of the shopping list. Despite the rise of the hypermarket, specialist shops are still an important part of French life. The different shops dedicated to cheeses which have been matured by *affineurs,* the home-made desserts, beautifully wrapped chocolates, breads of many kinds, fish and other meats and wines testify to the French people's love of fine food.

Street scene with pavement produce, Beuzeville

## TYPES OF SHOPS

**Boucherie:** the butcher's shop, where everything but pork is sold (by tradition, the *charcuterie* handles pork). Closed: Mondays.

**Boucherie chevaline:** the horse's head outside shows that this is a horse butcher. Open: Mondays.

**Boulangerie:** perhaps the most important of all, since the French buy their bread fresh twice a day for lunch and dinner. The long, familiar loaf is a *baguette* but *pain complet* (wholemeal bread) is common nowadays, as is *pain de campagne,* a heavy white country bread, or *pain de seigle,* a slightly sour rye bread, good with cheese. The sign 'depôt de pain' denotes shops that sell bread, but do not bake it.

**Charcuterie:** formerly the *charcutier* dealt only with the pig and its by-products such as sausages, terrines and *pâtés.* Nowadays this looks more and more like a delicatessen.

**Confiserie:** sells sweets made on the premises. Chocolates are always a feature and are always beautifully displayed and wrapped.

**Épicerie:** literally a spice shop, now the grocer's, carrying almost everything.

**Fromagerie:** the best cheese shops are run by *affineurs,* who mature cheeses they buy from the farmer and sell them at peak condition.

**Pâtisserie:** cake shops full of home-made tarts and ice cream, pastries and cakes. Many have home-made chocolates too.

**Poissonnerie:** the best fishmongers often smoke fish and make fish *pâtés* and fish soup.

**Traiteur:** ready-made dishes to take home.

**Triperie:** common in Normandy, where tripe is a popular delicacy, and often tastes better when cooked by a specialist.

**Volailler:** poulterers seem to be on the decline, since butchers often sell chickens and guinea fowl, roasting them in electric *rôtissoires* for instant take-aways.

## Where to find the best
### Lisieux

**Boulangerie Gilbert Heuzé** is the kind of bakery you'll dream of years later. Made entirely from scratch on the premises – the baguette de tradition is definitive, ready for a picnic. For dessert – bourdelot, chaussons au pommes and

tarts make the choice difficult.
*Avenue Victor-Hugo. Tel: 02 31 62 04 59.*

### Dieppe
**L'Épicier Olivier** is a delightful
delicatessen run by the brother of
Philippe Olivier, the famous cheese-shop
owner in Boulogne.
*16 rue Saint-Jacques. Tel: 02 35 84 22 55.*

### Étretat
The restored covered market has an
assortment of fun shops, including local
foods and gifts such as unusual candles.

### Honfleur
**La Paneterie** is rated as one of the finest
bakeries in Normandy, thanks to the
efforts of Louis David who bakes at least
15 different breads every day. Purists
insist on *pain brié*, a local heavy white
bread to accompany shrimps. You can
feel his seven-grain loaves doing you the
world of good.
*26 rue de la République.*
*Tel: 02 31 89 18 70.*

### Pont-Audemer
**Au Fromage Blanc** is the sort of shop
photographers love to spend time in,
with discs of real Camembert and
Livarot, the square Pont-l'Évêque and
cheeses from Bray. Good selection of
wines.
*78 rue de la République.*
*Tel: 02 32 41 06 79.*

### Pont-l'Évêque
**M Lemonnier** is an outstanding
*boulanger*, with a splendid selection of
breads and rolls for sale.
*1 rue St-Michel. Tel: 02 31 64 01 94.*

### Rouen
**Hardy** is one of the city's most famous
old *charcuteries*.
*22 place du Vieux Marché.*
*Tel: 02 35 71 81 55.*

Despite their love of food and
tradition, the French are also
conscious of the time and money
saved at supermarkets. The result
is the *hyper*, *hypermarché* or
hypermarket, the biggest shopping
arenas in Europe. The names are
splattered across advertising hoardings
for miles: Auchan, Carrefour,
Champion, Géant Casino, Euromarché,
Leclerc and Mammouth.

Signs like this one in Beuvron-en-Auge confirm the individual character of some establishments

## MARKETS

The Normans are great hagglers. That news may come as no comfort for non-French speakers, but a smile, a shrug and a pleading look could help drive a bargain in the markets that thrive all over Normandy.

As elsewhere in France, pride of place goes to food and local produce is of a very high standard: farm-reared chickens and rabbits, farm-made cheese and cider, farm-grown potatoes and carrots, farm-bottled honey and jam.

The markets are usually held once a week. Local farmers and their wives are regulars, as are itinerant salespeople who follow a circuit with van-loads of clothes, shoes, baskets and kitchenware. You see them day after day in market after market. Typical country markets, like those below, are morning-only affairs.

**L'Aigle**
Tuesday; one of France's largest, with over 1,000 animals and local produce.
**Alençon**
Tuesday, Thursday, Saturday and Sunday.
**Avranches**
Saturday.
**Barneville**
Saturday.
**Carteret**
Thursday in summer.
**Bayeux**
Saturday, place St-Patrice.
**Bernay**
Saturday.
**Cabourg**
Wednesday, Sunday in winter. Daily during July, August.
**Caen**
Friday, place St-Sauveur; Sunday, place Courtonne.

Norman markets are full of excellent fresh produce . . .

. . . but get there early for the very best

**Caudebec-en-Caux**
Saturday.
**Cherbourg**
Fish: daily, except on Sunday; on
Sunday, go to avenue de Normandie,
Octeville.
**Coutances**
Thursday.
**Dieppe**
Saturday.
**Étretat**
Thursday.
**Fécamp**
Saturday.
**Lisieux**
Saturday; large market with mostly
local producers, and a lovely, friendly
atmosphere.
**Livarot**
Thursday.

**Lyons-la-Forêt**
Thursday.
**Mortagne-sur-Perche**
Saturday.
**Pont-Audemer**
Monday; also Sunday in summer.
**Pont-l'Évêque**
Monday.
**St-Lô**
Saturday.
**Ste-Mère-Église**
Thursday.
**St-Vaast-la-Hougue**
Saturday.
**Sées**
Saturday.
**Villedieu-les-Poêles**
Tuesday.
**Vimoutiers**
Monday (cattle), Friday.

## FARMHOUSE FARE

One of the great delights in Normandy is going to see cheeses being made, cider being bottled or calvados distilled . . . then buying from the man or woman who produced them. Here is a selection where visitors are welcome. For cheesemakers, morning is the best time to catch a glimpse of the artisans at work. Don't be worried if your French is not fluent: an interest in good food transcends language barriers.

### Cheese
#### Camembert

François Durand's Ferme de la Héronnière is the last to make farmhouse AOC camembert, and they have a visitors' circuit so you can watch. *Open: Mon–Sat, standard hours. Tel: 02 33 39 08 08.*

#### Boissey

At Les Fromagers de Traditions, at La Houssaye, they not only make superlative cheeses (Livarot, Pont-

Choose your cheese with care

l'Évêque, Pavé d'Auge) in the old-fashioned way, but sell them direct to the public at weekdays. *Tel: 02 31 20 64 00.*

#### Crèvecœur

The Domaine de St-Loup specialises in Camembert in St-Loup-de-Fribois, just outside Crèvecœur. *Tel: 02 31 63 04 04.*

#### Lessay

See the traditional manufacture of award-winning REO camembert, with free tasting sessions. *Open: July–mid-Sept, Mon–Fri, standard hours; rest of the year by advance arrangement. Tel: 02 33 46 41 33.*

#### Livarot

Graindorge is synonymous with quality Pont-l'Évêque and Livarot cheeses. *Open: Mon–Fri, standard hours; Sat, mornings only. Tel: 02 31 48 20 10.*

Produce fresh from the farm

### St-Hilaire-Petitville

Eric Robert makes cheeses at the Chevrerie du Mesnil in the Cotentin marshes. Call ahead to make sure they are home.
*Tel: 02 33 42 32 00.*

### Cider and Calvados makers
### Crouttes

Just outside Vimoutiers, the Olivier family make excellent *pommeau*, as well as cider and calvados in an old farmhouse.
*La Galotière. Tel: 02 33 39 05 98.*

### Amaye-sur-Seulles

In the heart of Calvados, Le Clos d'Orval shows visitors how apple-based drinks are made. With 20 hectares (49 acres) of apple orchards, M. Aubrée produces cider and apple juice, *pommeau*, calvados and apple vinegar. A tour includes a visit to the cellars, a tasting and entry to a small museum.

Tiled sign of Livarot cheese makers

*Open: Mon–Sat, standard hours.*
*Orval. Tel: 02 31 77 02 87.*

### Dampierre

The Lair family have old agricultural implements, as well as tastings for sparkling cider and calvados.
*Le Pressoir Dajon.*
*Tel: 02 31 68 72 30.*

It's tempting to buy just for the labels . . .

If you're looking for antiques, Normandy is an excellent hunting ground

## SPECIALITY SHOPPING

Caen, Le Mans and Rouen have all the shops expected of sophisticated cities, from department stores to speciality boutiques, but there are also a handful of towns and villages still renowned for specific crafts.

For lace, head for the Musée des Beaux-Arts et de la Dentelle in Alençon or La Maison des Dentelles in Argentan (*see pp122–3*). Each town had a different *point* (stitch), while a third design is produced in Bayeux. Examples are sold at the lace school in the Hôtel du Doyen (*see p96*).

Also in Bayeux are the Ateliers d'Art de Bayeux, small shops in the place aux Pommes (near the new tourist office) which sell well-made reproductions of traditional lace, pottery and tapestry work.

*Vannerie* (basket-weaving) is still a feature of Remilly-sur-Lozon, a small village on the D8, off the D900 northwest of St-Lô. Bigger by far is Villedieu-les-Poêles, which lives up to its name: 'God's town of the frying pans'. Copper pots and pans are everywhere, coated with robust stainless steel or the more delicate tin that is preferred by chefs.

Another local tradition is salt-glaze pottery, made originally for workers to take cider to the fields or to transport butter. Noron-la-Poterie (*see p106*), southwest of Bayeux, is the centre of this craft where you can watch potters at work at the Atelier Turgis (*tel: 02 31 92 57 03*).

Rouen is known for its faïence, and reproductions of traditional designs are everywhere. Near the church of St-Maclou is the Carpentier workshop and shop which continues the 400-year-old tradition of hand-painting (*26 rue St-Romain, tel: 02 35 88 77 47*). All around this medieval area, the Quartier St-Maclou, are antiques shops, rivalled only by the rue St-Pierre in Caen.

## Antiques

Normandy is famous for the richness and depth of its antiques trade. As well as shops, regular auctions take place at the Salle or Hôtel des Ventes (public auction room).

Parisians like nothing better on a weekend than to poke around the *marchés des puces* (flea markets) looking for bargains. For foreign visitors, these can often be the source of an unusual souvenir.

Look out for the Salons des Antiquaires or Brocanteurs (antiques or bric-a-brac fair), or a 'Foire à Tout' or 'Vide Grenier', the equivalent of a car boot sale or garage sale.

**Duclair:** Sunday afternoon in the Salle des Ventes.

**Granville:** auctions every weekend, but check which day (*tel: 02 33 40 03 01*).

**Le Mans:** Friday morning, the flea market is in the avenue de Paderborn below the cathedral.

**Nogent-le-Rotrou:** the Saturday auction is held in the Hôtel des Ventes du Perche.

**Rouen:** some 100 sellers gather at the Clos St-Marc each weekend near the church of St-Maclou. It would be wise to get there early. The Thursday flea market is a tradition at the place des Emmurées, muddled in with the usual food and vegetable market. In the third week of October, one of France's largest antiques fairs is in the Parc des Expositions.

**Vire:** public sales at the Hôtel des Ventes on Saturday afternoons.

Gleaming copper in a specialist shop at Villedieu-les-Poêles

# Entertainment

Entertainment in Normandy does not revolve around theatre and opera. With such a rural tradition, Normans get together at horse fairs and cattle sales for festivals of herring and agricultural shows. The weekly market is as much a social as a commercial event.

A café rendezvous

As for music, there are concerts and recitals in many of the famous churches and abbeys, while summer brings the jazz festival at the Abbaye de l'Épau near Le Mans and the Semaines Musicales (musical weeks) in Fécamp.

Also in summer you can enjoy **Les Imaginaires du Mont-St-Michel**.

These are not guided tours; the visitors can stroll informally through crypt, cloister and church, where light, shadow and music combine to create a special experience.
*Tel: 02 33 60 14 30.*
*Open: early June–Sept, Mon–Sat, nights.*
*Admission charge.*

Deauville's elegant casino oozes refinement

Casino elegance and beach-side leisure at Trouville

## Casinos

Good restaurants, discos and floor shows complement the gambling facilities in many French casinos. All of them are open year round.

The most popular game is *boule*, which is generally known as '*la roulette des pauvres*' (roulette for the poor). There are only nine numbers; if you can put your *jeton* (chip) on the right number, you can get back seven times your *mise* (stake). Red or black, odd or even pays even money. There is a minimum stake as well as a maximum in most casinos.

## Deauville

The most famous casino of them all, the **Casino Barrière de Deauville** is the *Casino Royale* of the James Bond book. Slot machines, *boule*, baccarat, roulette, blackjack and chemin-de-fer.
*Rue Edmond Blanc.*
*Tel: 02 31 14 31 14.*

## Ouistreham–Riva-Bella

At Le Queen Normandy: *boule*, slot machines, nightclub, billiards.
*Place Alfred Thomas.*
*Tel: 02 31 36 30 00.*

## Trouville-sur-Mer

Blackjack, roulette, *boule*, craps, 200 slot machines.
*Place du Maréchal Foch.*
*Tel: 02 31 87 75 00.*

summer, this is the Monte Carlo of the North.

**Toujours le sport**

Sailors come in June for regattas, followed by the racing and horsey crowd at Clairefontaine Racecourse in July and La Touques in August. Bridge lovers and musicians are also July visitors, while the polo World Championship is an August highlight. In September, the film industry invades again, for the Festival of American Films. Throughout the 'season', wealthy families from Paris move in, as they have since the railway arrived in 1863: mother and children are joined by father for the weekends. No wonder the nicknames of *Tout-Paris-sur-Mer* (Paris Society-by-the-Sea) or the *21st arrondissement* are popular.

Eating lunch round the pool at the Hôtel Royal, meeting in the piano-bar at the Normandy or working out at the Hôtel du Golf: celebrities who like to see and be seen at Deauville know where to go. Words like 'elegant' and 'luxurious', 'royalty' and 'film stars' always describe Deauville because, during the

## Start time

The jet set hovers around the three major hotels. The Normandy has hosted the film stars, ever since Claude Lelouch used this oversized grey-and-white Norman cottage as the backdrop to his 1966 film, *Un Homme et une Femme* – don't be surprised to see Alain Delon in that bar. The old money stays at the Royal, and has done for decades. Racehorse owners and polo players abound, though Kevin Kline and Rosanna Arquette have been spotted in the bar. Out at the Hôtel du Golf with its 27-hole course and tennis courts, racing driver Jean-Pierre Jabouille might rub shoulders with tennis star Henri Leconte. There are balls and dinners, nights spent at the Casino, whose tall windows hide over 200 slot machines, plus the strictly formal Rotonde Restaurant and Régine's nightclub alongside the palatial *salles des jeux* (gambling rooms). Many celebrities have no need of hotels: couturier Yves Saint Laurent holds court in his seaside mansion; actor Gérard Depardieu lives down the road.

Late risers sip black coffee at Le Bar de la Mer *sur les planches*, then order a seafood lunch nearby at Le Bar du Soleil. At Le Ciro's, those in the know ask to see the *Livre d'Or*, the visitors' book, to decipher the autographs of the rich and famous. It's all part of the Deauville season, which lasts for a frantic, fun-filled 100 days.

If you want to glimpse a famous face, then Deauville in the season could be a good place

# Children

Although Normandy is rich with history, it is still a popular family destination, and there are plenty of attractions for younger children when the weather keeps them off the beach. The region is particularly rich in wildlife parks.

Ceiling in the Château de Balleroy reflects its ballooning connections

Many of these parks are seasonal attractions, open during school holidays. Check before setting off.

### Château de Balleroy
**The Musée des Ballons** (Balloon Museum) reflects France's role in the invention of the *montgolfière* (hot-air balloon). Festival of balloons in June.
*15km (9 miles) southwest of Bayeux, off the D572. Tel: 02 31 21 60 61;*
*www.chateau-balleroy.com*
*Open: July–Aug, daily; Mar–June & Sept–mid-Oct, Mon–Fri. Admission charge.*

### Lisieux
An intact manorial compound, Domaine de St Hoppolyte is a farm-museum that focuses on the living, active parts of Norman farms that survive. A herd of Norman cows grazes under apple trees, their milk made into cheese on-site. Texts explain ecosystem, techniques, and architecture.
*Just south of Lisieux on D579. Tel: 02 31 31 30 68. Open: May–Sept, daily; Oct–Apr, Mon–Fri, standard hours (see pp186–7). Admission charge.*

### Beauvoir
This **reptilarium** has 200 snakes and crocodiles from all over the world.

*5km (3 miles) south of Mont-St-Michel. Tel: 02 33 68 11 18. Open: daily in summer; daily, afternoons in winter. Closed: Jan, Mon–Fri. Admission charge.*

### Caen-Carpiquet
**Festyland** is a typical amusement park complete with radio-controlled cars, slides and miniature train.
*Just west of Caen, off the N13. Tel: 02 31 75 04 04. Open: Mar–Sept, daily. Admission charge.*

### Caudebec-en-Caux
The **Musée de la Marine de Seine** records the importance of transport on this major river. Good audiovisual display. Many old boats, carefully restored, including a *gribane*, a river transport boat with sails.
*35km (22 miles) west of Rouen, on the D982. Tel: 02 35 95 90 13. Open: daily, afternoons. Admission charge.*

### Champrépus
The **parc zoologique** (zoo) has nearly 100 species of animals scattered over 6 hectares (15 acres).
*8km (5 miles) west of Villedieu-les-Poêles, on the D924. Tel: 02 33 61 30 74. Open: Apr–Oct, daily. Closed: mornings in winter. Admission charge.*

## Clécy

The **Musée du Chemin de Fer Miniature** (model railway museum) is devoted to model and miniature railways with rides (*see pp74–5*).
*At Les Fours à Chaux, 38km (24 miles) southeast of Caen, on the D562. Tel: 02 31 69 07 13. Open: Easter–Sept, daily; Mar–Easter, Oct, Sun afternoons. Admission charge.*

## Clères

This **parc zoologique** is one of the biggest and best in France. Animals including flamingoes, emus, kangaroos and antelopes roam freely in the grounds of the Château de Clères.
*16km (10 miles) due north of Rouen, off the N27. Tel: 02 35 33 23 08. Open: mid-Mar–Nov, daily. Admission charge.*

## Courseulles

On the seafront, the **Maison de la Mer** aquarium offers a journey through its glass tunnel to view life under the sea. The fine shell collection is also worth visiting.
*18km (11 miles) northeast of Caen, on the D514. Tel: 02 31 37 92 58. Open: Feb–Sept, daily, standard hours (see pp186–7); Oct, Nov, Jan, daily, afternoons. Admission charge.*

## Étretat

The **Parc de Loisir des Roches** (the Roches Leisure Park) has pools, pedaloes, inflatable castles and mini golf. The **Aquarium Marin** (Marine Aquarium) at the far end of the park has tropical fish as well as local species.
*28km (17 miles) north of Le Havre, via the D940. Tel: 02 35 29 80 59. Open: Apr–mid-June, Sat, Sun, Wed, afternoons; mid-June–Sept, daily, afternoons. Admission charge.*

Peacock and little girl sizing each other up in the park at Clères

## La Ferté-Macé

The **Musée du Jouet** (Toy Museum) brings together toys from the past 100 years and some early sound recordings on wax cylinders.

*Rue de la Victoire, in La Ferté-Mace 46km (29 miles) northwest of Alençon, on the D916. Tel: 02 33 37 04 08.*
*Open: Apr–June & Sept–Oct, Sat & Sun, afternoons; July–Aug, daily, afternoons. Admission charge.*

## Fleury-la-Forêt

The **Château de Fleury** has a collection of dolls, including a 3-m (10-ft) tall dolls' house and dolls riding a miniature roundabout.

*40km (25 miles) east of Rouen, in Lyons Forest. Tel: 02 32 49 54 34. Open: Easter–Oct, daily. Admission charge.*

## Gisors

The **Parc de Loisirs du Bois d'Hérouval** (Hérouval Leisure Park) is 4km (2$^1$/$_2$ miles) from Gisors on the Pontoise road. With 100 attractions ranging from water-slides to a miniature train.

*57km (35 miles) southeast of Rouen, on the D14. Tel: 02 32 55 33 76. Open: Easter–Aug, daily. Admission charge.*

## Granville

One ticket covers three attractions: the **Aquarium Marin du Roc**, **Palais Minéral** and **Jardin des Papillons**. You can see insects, fish, butterflies, and the famous 'sculptures' and 'paintings' made entirely from shells.

*105km (65 miles) south of Cherbourg, off the D971. Tel: 02 33 50 19 83. Open: mid-Apr–mid-Sept, daily. Admission charge.*

## Grimbosq

The **Forêt de Grimbosq** contains a wildlife park concentrating on animals native to the region.

*16km (10 miles) southwest of Caen, on the D562. Tel: 02 31 30 41 00.*
*Open: Apr–Nov, daily; mid-Nov–Mar, Sat, Sun & Wed, afternoons. Free admission.*

## Le Havre

The *Le Havre III* fireship floats alongside the **Musée Maritime et Portuaire** and is part of the story of merchant shipping.

*La Pointe de Floride. Tel: 02 35 24 51 00.*
*Open: Sun, Mon & Wed, afternoons. Admission charge.*

## Hermival-les-Vaux

More than 250 African animals roam free in the 50-hectare (124-acre) **Parc Zoologique Cerzá**, a zoo near Lisieux. There is also a breeding centre for rare species.

*9km (5$^1$/$_2$ miles) northeast of Lisieux, on the D510. Tel: 02 31 62 17 22.*
*Open: daily. Closed: Dec–Jan. Admission charge.*

## Honfleur

Overlooking the old port, the Église St-Étienne is a 14th-century church housing a good **Musée de la Marine** (marine museum).

*15km (9 miles) northeast of Deauville, on the coast. Tel: 02 31 89 14 12.*
*Open: Apr–Sept, Tue–Sun, standard hours; mid-Feb–Mar & Oct–mid-Nov, Tue–Fri, afternoons, Sat–Sun, standard hours (see pp186–7). Admission charge.*

Alongside the church above, the **Musée d'Ethnographie et d'Art Populaire** re-creates the traditional Normandy of yesteryear. Among the dozen rooms are a kitchen with shiny copper pans and a workshop.
*Rue de la Prison. Open: same as the Musée de la Marine. Admission charge.*

### Le Mans
**Musée de l'Automobile**, the car museum next to the Le Mans motor racing circuit, has high-tech displays alongside vintage models.
*Tel: 02 43 72 72 24. Open: daily. Closed: Oct–May, Tue. Admission charge.*

### Montaigu-la-Brisette
The **Parc Zoologique St. Martin** is a wildlife park with a selection of unusual animals from five continents.
*Between Valognes and St-Vaast-la-Hougue, on the D902. Tel: 02 33 40 40 98. Open: June–Aug, daily; out of season, Sun & bank holiday, afternoons. Admission charge.*

### Mortain
The **Village Enchanté**, the Magic Village at Bellefontaine, is both a leisure park and a nature reserve. As well as fairy-tale scenes for smaller children, there is an adventure playground. A model train does the rounds of this fairyland village, which has the added attraction of a puppet theatre. Very popular.
*5km (3 miles) northwest of Mortain, on the D33. Tel: 02 33 59 01 93. Open: Easter–Sept, daily. Admission charge.*

### Plasnes
The **Parc des Oiseaux** is a huge bird-life centre with large aviaries, as well as reptiles, dinosaur replicas and games. It is set in the forest 4km (2¹/₂ miles) from Bernay on the RN138. There are magic shows on Sunday afternoons.
*Tel: 02 32 43 21 22. Open: mid-Mar–end-Sept, daily. Admission charge.*

### St-Vaast-la-Hougue
The island of Tatihou just off the coast now has a **maritime museum** in the 17th-century fortifications. Cross by boat.
*Tel: 02 33 23 19 92.*
*Open: May–Sept, daily; Oct–Apr, Sat & Sun. Admission charge.*

### Trouville
The **Aquarium Écologique** is one of France's biggest and best aquariums. More than 20 years old, it boasts mangrove swamps and Amazon rain-forest to show off the species in natural habitats, 75 tanks of fish, including several varieties of shark, and a selection of creepy-crawlies and reptiles.
*17 rue de Paris. Tel: 02 31 88 46 04. Open: daily. Admission charge.*

**Club Mickey** offers beach games, sports, tennis and swimming for children from 3 to 13 years of age.
*Promenade des Planches. Tel: 02 31 88 15 04. Open: daily in summer. Admission charge.*

### Villerville
**Mer et Désert** complements the aquarium at Trouville with hundreds of live shellfish and cacti.
*Between Deauville and Honfleur, on the D513. Tel: 02 31 81 13 81. Open: Easter–Oct, daily, afternoons. Admission charge.*

# Sport and leisure

Fishing in an incomparable setting: on the Seine at Les Andelys

Normandy is scarcely a hotbed of sport when it comes to team games like football or basketball. Normans are great individualists; they love horses and horse-racing; many would die to be a great cyclist. One of the sport's legends was Jacques Anquetil, who dominated the cycling Tour de France at his peak, winning in 1957 and then 1961 to 1964. Never a showy rider, he ground his opponents down with steady, well-planned riding: gritty and typically Norman.

One of the start points for the 2002 Tour de France was St Martin des Landelles, near Avranches. The boom in recent years has been golf, catering to the rise in interest across France but also to British, Dutch and German visitors looking for golf without queues.

There are also plenty of opportunities for biking, riding and walking. Renting a *vélo* (bicycle) or VTT (mountain bike) is easy: hire from bike shops, or even from SNCF railway stations at Bayeux, Cabourg, Dives, Fécamp, Le Tréport, Pontorson, Sillé-le-Guillaume, Trouville-Deauville and Vernon. Each *département* has permanent cycle trails that are clearly marked.

Hiking trails, too, abound, often linking in to France's national network, the Sentiers de Grande Randonnée, or GR for short. The GR2 runs along the Seine Valley, the GR21 traces the Lézarde Valley and the GR221 cuts through the Suisse Normande. Panoramic views and brisk breezes are a feature of the GR22/223 which follows the coast of the Cotentin Peninsula between Mont-St-Michel and Barfleur.

## HORSE RIDING

A list of approved establishments is downloadable as a PDF at *www.ffe.com*, available from the **Comité Régionale de Tourisme Équestre**.
*Centre Equestre Poney Club, 27800 Le Bec Hellouin. Tel: 02 32 44 86 31.*

## SEA FISHING

Visitors to Normandy have the best of all worlds: sea fishing, fly fishing and coarse fishing. A *gaule* is a fishing rod, a *mouche* is a fly.

Listed here is a selection of the best places to fish. The telephone numbers are for the local fishing associations which look after licences and equipment hire. The brochure *Pêche en Normandie* is available from: Comité Régional de Tourisme de Normandie,
*14 rue Charles Corbeau, 27000 Évreux. Tel: 02 32 33 79 00.*

A knowledge of French is essential, so some names of fishes are given here:

| | |
|---|---|
| *Anguille:* eel | *Dorade:* bream |
| *Bars:* bass | *Mulet:* mullet |
| *Cabillaud:* cod | *Raie:* skate |
| *Congre:* conger eel | *Requin:* shark. |

## Courseulles

Surf casting for bass and mullet is popular; at the end of the season, in October and November, turbot is available.
*Boat hire tel: 02 31 37 46 80.*

## Dieppe

Fish from the jetties for conger eels in autumn, from Berneval beach for bass, and from boats for large cod in autumn.
*Boat hire tel: 02 35 84 90 98/35 04 56 08.*

## Fécamp

Bass is plentiful and easily caught from the jetties in summer, big conger eels in the autumn.
*Boat hire tel: 02 32 28 40 29.*

## Grandcamp

Off the Pointe du Hoc for bass; flat fish in the Vire estuary.
*Boat hire tel: 02 31 22 64 15.*

## Granville

Between the Chausey Islands and the bay of Mont-St-Michel, skate and hammerhead sharks add to the variety.
*Boat hire tel: 02 33 50 37 80.*

## INLAND FISHING

The chalk streams that run down to the sea are famous for their fly-fishing rivers. The following fish are found: *brochet* (pike), *ombre* (grayling), *saumon* (salmon), *sandre* (pike-perch), *truite de mer* (sea trout).

## Bresle River

On Normandy's northern border, the Bresle is good for sea trout.
*Season: late Mar–early Oct.*
*Tel: 02 35 50 12 84.*

## Charentonne River

One of the best trout streams in Normandy.
*Tel: 02 32 45 00 28.*

## Iton River

Évreux is a well-known centre for fly fishing on an 8.5-km (5 1/4-mile) stretch of the Iton.
*Season: late Mar–early Oct.*
*Tel: 02 32 24 04 43.*

## Marais du Cotentin

Four rivers flow into what used to be called the *pays de l'anguille* (eel-country). Pike and pike-perch abound.
*Tel: 02 33 42 18 34.*

## Pont-Audemer

Some 6km (4 miles) of the River Risle, a classic chalk stream offers fair-sized trout.
*Tel: 02 32 41 08 21.*

## Sée River

Near Mont-St-Michel, this is one of Normandy's top rivers for salmon fishing.
*Season: early Mar–mid-Sept.*
*Tel: 02 33 49 21 47.*

## Sienne River

In the southern Manche, the Sienne is best known for its trout, pike and pike-perch.
*Season: early Mar–mid-Sept.*
*Tel: 02 33 61 02 47.*

## Touques River

France's best river for sea trout.
*Season: late Apr–late Oct.*
*Tel: 02 31 64 00 77.*

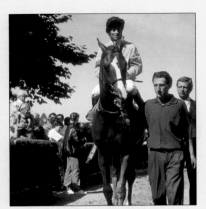

17th century that launched a national programme of breeding.

The stud at Haras du Pin opened in 1730. The Comte d'Artois (later Charles X) and the Prince de Lambesc went to study English breeding methods, and brought back two legendary stallions, Le Parfait and L'Aleyron. Their offspring were so successful that more stallions were imported; soon Normandy was the place to buy horses.

Although the network of national studs with their aristocratic connections was abolished after the French Revolution, Napoleon restored them, realising he needed quality cavalry mounts to support his incessant wars.

In the middle of the 19th century, the English passion for racing was matched by the French, whose greatest triumph was that of Gladiateur, who, in 1865, won the English Triple Crown (2000 Guineas, Derby and St Leger) as well as the Grand Prix de Paris.

Normandy's love affair with horses goes back centuries, to the days of the heavy horse used by farmers to plough their fields and by knights on the battlefield. During the Crusades, French knights were constantly outmanoeuvred by the swifter and more mobile Arab steeds. When this Arab blood was introduced to France, the quality of local horses improved dramatically.

As early as the 14th century, King Philip VI founded a stud near Domfront, but it was the initiative of Cardinal Richelieu and the minister to Louis XIV, Colbert, in the mid-

As well as the national studs of St-Lô and Haras du Pin, there are dozens in private ownership (over 1,200 in Calvados alone), easily

identified by the neat white fences and handsome brick stables.

While the thoroughbred racehorse receives the greatest publicity, Normandy also produces high-quality trotting horses and showjumpers, steeplechasers and hurdlers. Normandy's native breed is the Percheron, a heavy draught horse developed from the Belgian Brabant and Arab stock. It is very solidly built, often weighing about 1 tonne. Despite its short legs (with no long hair on the lower legs, unusual for a draught horse), it has a long stride and is good to ride. It is high-spirited and a willing worker, and has a heroic service record as a war horse.

The noble and massive Percherons have been given a new lease of life, delighting crowds as they pull carriages at exhibitions and on state occasions.

Facing page: the Deauville Grand Prix meeting is a much awaited event
Above: Percheron horses at Haras du Pin are easy to spot because of their magnificent size

## GOLF

Many regions of France have special golf passes, allowing golfers to play a different course each day. In the Calvados *département*, for example, visitors buying the Golf Pass can play six of the following courses over a period of nine days: Omaha Beach Golf Club; Golf de St-Gatien, Deauville; Golf de St-Julien; Golf de Cabourg le Home; Golf de Clécy-Cantelou; and Golf de Caen. The 'Golf Avantage' pass is available through Calvados Tourisme (*place du Canada, 14000 Caen, tel: 02 31 86 53 30*). The price is lower in the off season.

The encouragement for visitors can be gauged by the minimum handicap of 35 that is required to play the majority of golf courses in Normandy.

### Bagnoles-de-l'Orne

This elegant spa town needs more than a 9-hole course, but it provides a challenging round.
*Tel: 02 33 37 81 42.*

### Bellême

The 18-hole **Golf de Bellême St-Martin** attracts a lot of local youngsters.
*Tel: 02 33 73 00 07.*

### Cabourg

Near the spa at Varaville, the **Golf de Cabourg le Home** has 18 holes.
*Tel: 02 31 91 25 56.*

### Caen

The **Golf de Caen-Formule Golf** is at Biéville. 18 holes.
*Tel: 02 31 94 72 09.*

### Cherbourg

The **Association Sportive du Golf de Fontenay** has 9 holes.
*Tel: 02 33 21 44 27.*

### Clécy

The **Golf de Clécy** at the Manoir de Cantelou is a new 18-hole course.
*Tel: 02 31 69 72 72.*

### Deauville

The **New Golf Club** has been attracting the rich and famous since 1929. Twenty-seven holes plus luxury. *Tel: 02 31 80 21 53.*

**Golf de St-Gatien** at St-Gatien des Bois has both an 18- and a 9-hole course. *Tel: 02 31 65 19 99.*

**Golf Club de l'Amirauté** at Tourgeville is another new 18-hole course, popular in summer. *Tel: 02 31 14 42 00.*

### Dieppe

The **Golf de Dieppe** is the oldest course in Normandy, dating back to 1897.
*On the Route de Pourville.*
*Tel: 02 35 84 25 05.*

### Étretat

Another old course (1908), the **Marin d'Étretat** has spectacular views.
*Tel: 02 35 27 04 89.*

### Évreux

The **Golf Municipal** (18- and 9-hole courses) attracts enthusiastic youngsters.
*Tel: 02 32 39 66 22.*

### Forêt Verte

An 18-hole scenic course at Bose-Guérard St Adrien in the Seine Maritime *département*.

*Open: all year round.*
*Tel: 02 35 33 62 94.*

### Granville
The **Golf Club de Granville International** has been going since 1912 and has 27 holes.
*Open: all year.*
*Tel: 02 35 50 23 06.*

### Le Havre
The 18-hole **Golf du Havre**, out at Octeville-sur-Mer, 10km (6 miles) north of Le Havre, has been open for over 60 years.
*Tel: 02 35 46 36 50.*

### Le Mans
South of the city at Mulsanne, the **Le Golf Club du Mans** has 18 holes.
*Tel: 02 43 42 00 36.*

### Le Neubourg
The **Golf du Château du Champ-du-Bataille** is one of the best courses in the country, carved out of the woods surrounding the 18th-century château.

*Open: all year round.*
*Tel: 02 32 35 03 72.*

### Léry-Poses
The **Golf de Léry-Poses** is a new course in a leisure resort. 18 holes.
*Open: all year round.*
*Tel: 02 32 59 47 42.*

### Le Vaudreuil
The **Golf du Vaudreuil** is on an island in the Eure, near Louviers. This picturesque course, with its thatched clubhouse and 18th-century hotel, was designed by English golf guru Fred Hawtree.
*Tel: 02 32 59 02 60.*

### Omaha Beach
The **Omaha Beach Golf Club** with its 27 holes at Port-en-Bessin is a great success.
*Tel: 02 31 22 12 12.*

### Rouen
The **Rouen Golf Club** at Mont-St-Aignan is 3km (2 miles) from Rouen. 18 holes.
*Tel: 02 35 76 38 65.*

Tee-off practice in an idyllic setting

Both hard and grass courts offer a variety of tennis facilities

## SWIMMING, TENNIS AND LEISURE CENTRES

Even the smallest French village will have *camping* (campsite), *piscine* (swimming pool) and *tennis* (tennis courts) to attract holidaymakers. There has also been a growth in the *centres de loisirs*, which translates as leisure centres. Often on an artificial lake with a small beach of imported sand, these are ideal for families since they usually offer something for everyone, from pedaloes to fishing, windsurfing to tennis, or the favourite of the locals, a game of *boules* (French bowls). Some might have water-skiing and special instruction in canoeing or kayaking, a chance to rent mountain bikes or play tennis. There is usually a small café or restaurant.

### Brionne

There are lifeguards here in summer. *40km (25 miles) east of Lisieux, on the River Risle, off the N13. Tel: 02 32 43 66 11.*

### Cany-Barville

Water-skiing is possible on the Lac de Caniel. *20km (12 miles) east of Fécamp, on the D925. Tel: 02 35 97 40 55.*

### Conches

Tennis and pony rides are among the land-based activities at the Domaine de la Nöé. Summer only. *18km (11 miles) southwest of Évreux, on the D830. Tel: 02 32 37 61 97.*

### Dangu

With its campsite, this is popular with families who can windsurf and canoe on Gisors Lake. *8km (5 miles) southwest of Gisors, on the D181. Tel: 02 32 55 43 42.*

### La Ferté-Macé
Based around a huge lake with an imported sandy beach.
*46km (28¹/₂ miles) northwest of Alençon, on the D916. Tel: 02 33 37 47 00.*

### Grosley-sur-Risle
Visitors have to bring their own windsurfers and canoes, but there is micro-light flying for the daring.
*7km (4 miles) south of Beaumont-le-Roger, on the River Risle.*
*Tel: 02 32 46 25 28.*

### Jumièges-le-Mesnil
A wide-ranging array of adventure sports, include climbing, catamarans and archery.
*27km (17 miles) west of Rouen, near the River Seine. Tel: 02 35 37 93 84.*

### Le Mêle-sur-Sarthe
Watersports and tennis.
*20km (12 miles) northeast of Alençon, on the N12. Tel: 02 33 27 61 02.*

### Pont-l'Évêque
A huge lake for watersports, plus tennis, riding and cycling.
*47km (29 miles) northeast of Caen, off the A13. Tel: 02 31 64 23 93.*

### Poses
The Léry-Poses centre is known for its golf course, water-skiing and campsite.
*16km (10 miles) southwest of Rouen, on south bank of the River Seine. Tel: 02 32 59 13 13.*

### Toutainville
Above-average instruction available at the Centre Nautique for sail sports.
*5km (3 miles) west of Pont-Audemer, on the N175. Tel: 02 32 41 13 05.*

### Vimoutiers
Youngsters enjoy learning to ride at the Escale du Vitou, which has a swimming pool as well as a lake.
*27km (17 miles) south of Lisieux, on the D579. Tel: 02 33 39 12 05.*

Children learning to sail at Le Havre

# Food and drink

Three ingredients seem to dominate menus in Normandy: cream, apples and seafood. These are made into cheese and butter, cider and calvados, which are cooked with a huge variety of fish and shellfish to present a delicious range of dishes. Beef dominates inland menus, ideally grilled as simple steaks or made into peasant dishes.

Hand-made *andouille* and its accompaniment, fine cider, at Vire

Each area has its specialities, from the duck of Rouen and nearby Duclair to the *pré-salé* lamb of the Mont-St-Michel salt marshes. Tripe is an acquired taste, whether it is served *à la mode de Caen* in a restaurant, or on a skewer from a market stall. Vegetarians will find themselves frustrated, as even salads often contain pork lardons or other meat products. Many restaurants do offer a salad with local cheeses, however, and crêperies are your best bet for finding variety. A cheese board should always contain Normandy's cheeses: Camembert, Pont-l'Évêque, Liverot and Neufchatel. Many desserts include apples or a dash of calvados with a bowl of cream. The following are some local names and dishes:

**andouilles de Vire:** usually *fumées* (smoked), chitterlings or tripe sausages.
**andouillettes***:* smaller tripe sausages, grilled and served hot.
**anguilles:** eels; sometimes in pâtés.
**assiette anglaise:** assorted cold meats/ sausage served as a starter.
**barbue:** brill; often served *à l'oseille*, in a sorrel sauce.
**beignet:** doughnut or fritter.
**bigorneaux:** winkles.

**boudin blanc:** white sausage made with white meat such as chicken and pork.
**boudin noir:** black pudding, sausage made with pig's blood.
**bourdelot:** whole apple baked in pastry.
**brioche:** light, sweet bun made with yeast, butter and eggs.
**buccins:** whelks.
**cabillaud:** fresh cod; *morue* is salted.
**café calva:** black coffee with calvados.
**caïeu (d'Isigny):** the large mussels from the bay of Isigny.
**caneton:** duck, duckling. When served *à la rouennaise*, Rouen-style, this duck has pink flesh, as it is strangled to keep the blood. The sauce is very rich.
**carotte:** carrot.
**cassis:** blackcurrant.
**céleri:** celery.
**céleri-rave:** celeriac: the root is grated and often appears alongside grated carrot in salads as *céleri rémoulade*.
**champignon:** mushroom.
**chaussons aux pommes:** apple turnover.
**chou:** cabbage.
**chou-fleur:** cauliflower.
**ciboulette:** chives.
**colin:** hake; when served *à la granvillaise*, the sauce has shrimps in it.
**crevette:** shrimp.
**criste-marine:** samphire.

**déca/décaféiné:** decaffeinated.

**demoiselles (de Cherbourg):** often large prawns, but should be small lobsters.

**douillon:** pear baked in pastry.

**Duchesses de Rouen:** macaroons.

**échalotes:** shallots.

**estragon:** tarragon; *à l'estragon*, with a tarragon sauce.

**farci:** stuffed.

**ficelle normande:** stuffed pancake (cheese, ham, mushrooms) in a cream sauce.

**fouace:** a sweet cake.

**fraises:** strawberries; *des bois*, wild.

**fruits de mer:** a mixed platter of fresh shellfish.

**gâche:** flat, brioche-like breakfast bun.

**gades:** local name for gooseberries.

**gâteau de Trouville:** a cake filled with cream and apples.

**gibier:** game.

**groseilles:** redcurrants.

**groseilles à maquereau:** gooseberries, so-called for their striped surface resembling mackerel.

**hareng:** herring.

**huîtres:** oysters.

    **creuses:** the large Japanese variety.

    **plates belons:** the native oyster.

    **claires:** higher class of oyster.

    **fines de claires:** very high-class oyster, allowed to fatten up in a special *claire* or salt marsh.

**jambon:** ham; *au cidre*, cooked in cider.

**lait:** milk.

**laitue:** lettuce.

**lapereau, lapin:** rabbit.

**lisette:** young mackerel.

**maquereau:** mackerel.

**marmite dieppoise:** a *marmite* is an old-fashioned cooking pot, but this is a fish stew made with cream, white wine and mushrooms.

**matelote normande:** a sea-fish stew.

**merlan:** whiting.

**mirlitons (de Rouen):** a cream puff.

**morue:** salt cod.

**moules:** mussels; *à la marinière*, cooked in white wine, with shallots, herbs and butter; *à la normande*, with cream added to above; buchot, a local variety.

**navets:** turnips.

**oignons:** onions.

**omelette Mère Poulard:** named after the inventor whose restaurant on Mont-St-Michel is legendary. A light, spongy omelette where whites and yolks are beaten separately before mixing.

**omelette normande:** could be either with cream, calvados and apples (dessert) or with shrimps and mushrooms (starter).

**palourdes:** clams.

**parfum:** flavour (as in ice cream).

**persil:** parsley.

**poireaux:** leeks.

**pommes de terre:** potatoes, often *vapeur* (steamed).

**poulet Vallée d'Auge:** chicken cooked with cream and cider, even apples.

**praires:** small clams.

**radis:** radish.

**rabote:** apple baked in pastry.

**sablé:** shortbread-like biscuit.

**salade cauchoise:** with potato salad, chopped ham and celery.

**sole:** sole; *à la dieppoise*, in a white wine, cream and mushroom sauce; often with cream and calvados sauce; *normande*, with cream and cider sauce.

**tarte normande:** apple tart.

**tergoule:** rice pudding with cinnamon (also *tord-goule*).

**tripes:** tripe; *à la mode de Caen*, cooked with cider, calvados and root vegetables.

## Where to eat

In the following listing of recommended restaurants the star rating indicates the approximate cost per person for a meal, in euros.

★★      under €50
★★★    €50–€70
★★★★   over €70

### Alençon
**Le Bistrot ★★**
A 1930s' look, bistro fare.
*21 rue Sarthe.*
*Tel: 02 33 26 51 69.*

### Les Andelys
**La Chaîne d'Or ★★★★**
Classic French dishes in a pretty, old inn overlooking the Seine.
*27 rue Grande.*
*Tel: 02 32 54 00 31.*

### Bagnoles-de-l'Orne
**Manoir du Lys ★★★**
Posh hotel restaurant serving local lamb, *crêpes* with apples, even *escargots.*
*Rte de Juvigny.*
*Tel: 02 33 37 80 69.*

### Barneville-Carteret
**Les Isles ★★**
Fish dishes served on a terrace by the sea.
*9 boulevard Maritime.*
*Tel: 02 33 04 90 76.*

### La Marine ★★
Lobster, lamb and turbot; pretty views.
*11 rue de Paris.*
*Tel: 02 33 53 83 31.*

### Bayeux
**Le Lion d'Or ★★★**
Overlooking courtyard of old coaching inn: classic Norman dishes.
*71 rue St-Jean.*
*Tel: 02 31 92 06 90.*

### Bénouville
**Manoir d'Hastings ★★★**
Famous restaurant that now seems old-fashioned despite its appetising local food.

This street announces its varied gastronomic delights

*18 ave Côte-de-Nacre.*
*Tel: 02 31 44 62 43.*

### Beuvron-en-Auge
**Le Pavé d'Auge ★★**
Restored market building
in pretty village; good
local dishes.
*Place du Village.*
*Tel: 02 31 79 26 71.*

### Brouains
**Auberge du Moulin ★★★**
Old mill beside the River
Sée, serving excellent
local food and wine.
*Le Moulin de Brouains.*
*Tel: 02 33 59 50 60.*

### Caen
**La Bourride ★★★★**
Arguably the best
Normandy-style cooking
in the region in a fine
ancient restaurant.
*15 rue du Vaugeux.*
*Tel: 02 31 93 50 76.*

### Carentan
**Auberge Normande ★★**
Flowery, red-brick
roadside inn; serves
excellent local produce.
*17 blvd Verdun.*
*Tel: 02 33 42 28 28.*

### Cherbourg
**Le Faitout ★★**
Busy little bistro, plenty
of seafood, good desserts.
*Rue Tour-Carré.*
*Tel: 02 33 04 25 04.*

### Clécy
**Le Moulin du Vey ★★★**
Country-style hotel and
restaurant in the heart of
Suisse Normande by the
River Orne.
*Le Vey.*
*Tel: 02 31 69 71 08.*

### Colleville-Montgomery
**La Ferme
Saint-Hubert ★★**
Traditional dishes from
all over France pack in
visitors to the seaside.
*3 rue Mer.*
*Tel: 02 31 96 35 41.*

### Cuves
**Le Moulin de Jean ★★★**
Founded by famous chef
Jean-Christophe Novelli,
and still bears his
influence.
*La Lande, Cuves.*
*Tel: 02 33 48 39 29.*

### Deauville
**Le Ciro's ★★★★**
Where the superstars
lunch and dine in
season, overlooking
the sea.
*Blvd Mer.*
*Tel: 02 31 14 31 31.*

**Le Spinnaker ★★★★**
Up-market Norman
dishes include *bourdelot*,
apple baked in pastry.
*52 rue Mirabeau.*
*Tel: 02 31 88 24 40.*

### Dieppe
**Le Restaurant au
Port ★★★**
A real, old-fashioned fish
restaurant right by the
old harbour.
*99 Quai Henri IV.*
*Tel: 02 35 84 36 64.*

### Dives-sur-Mer
**Guillaume le
Conquérant ★★★**
Across the river from
Cabourg, up-market
restaurant in Louis XIV
style, in the centre of its
namesake's village.
*2 rue d'Hastings.*
*Tel: 02 31 91 07 26.*

### Évreux
**Hôtel de France ★★★**
Elegant hotel-restaurant
in the heart of town.
*29 rue St-Thomas.*
*Tel: 02 32 39 09 25.*

### Falaise
**Château du Tertre ★★★★**
Luxury country-house
hotel restaurant with only
the best.
*St-Martin-de-Mieux.*
*Tel: 02 31 90 01 04.*

### Fécamp
**La Marine ★★★**
A nice view of the port.
*Choucroute de la mer* is a
speciality.
*23 quai Vicomte.*
*Tel: 02 35 28 15 94.*

## Giverny
**La Musardière ★★★**
Hotel serving *crêpes* and
traditional cuisine, near
Claude Monet's house.
*Rue Claude Monet.*
*Tel: 02 32 21 03 18.*

## Granville
**La Gentilhommière ★★★**
Modern versions of
Norman recipes under
ancient beams.
*152 rue Couraye.*
*Tel: 02 33 50 17 99.*

Restaurant sign in Honfleur

## Le Havre
**La Petite Auberge ★★★**
Modern versions of old
Norman dishes; popular
with locals.
*32 rue Ste-Adresse.*
*Tel: 02 35 46 27 32.*

## Honfleur
**L'Assiette
Gourmande ★★★**
Chef Bonnefoy creates
some daring dishes with
fine local products.
*2 quai des Passagers.*
*Tel: 02 31 89 24 88.*

**La Ferme St-Siméon ★★★**
The cradle of the
Impressionist painters
is a high-quality hotel
restaurant today. One
that, quite appropriately,
serves only Norman
dishes.
*Rue Aldolphe-Marais.*
*Tel: 02 31 81 78 00.*

## Jumièges
**Auberge des Ruines ★★★**
Considering it looks
across at the abbey
ruins, the standards of
this restaurant are high
for the regular flow of
tourists.
*17 place de la Mairie.*
*Tel: 02 35 37 24 05.*

## Laval
**La Gerbe de Blé ★★★**
This hotel restaurant

sticks to old-fashioned
dishes and also boasts of
an excellent wine list – a
faultless formula for
attracting customers.
*83 rue Victor-Boissel.*
*Tel: 02 43 53 14 10.*

## Le Mans
**La Ciboulette ★★★**
Strictly for fish-lovers,
this trendy bistro is in the
old town.
*14 rue de la Vielle-Porte.*
*Tel: 02 43 24 65 67.*

## Le Sap
**Les Saveurs du Grand
Jardin ★★**
Fresh, light homage to
regional cuisine, with
particular attention to
vegetables; housed in a
rural life museum.
*Eco-musée, rue Grand
Jardin. Tel: 02 33 36 56 88.*

## Mont-St-Michel
**La Mère Poulard ★★★★**
This world-famous
restaurant survives the
hordes of tourists who
come to order the fluffy
omelettes.
*Grande Rue.*
*Tel: 02 33 60 14 01.*
**St-Pierre ★★**
This is another good
restaurant on the Mount,
and of excellent value.
*Grande Rue.*
*Tel: 02 33 60 14 03.*

### Mortain
**Au Bon Vent** ★★
Basic décor, but it has the best-quality main courses sandwiched between self-service entrées, cheese and desserts.
*64 rue du Rocher.*
*Tel: 02 33 59 00 68.*

### Orbec
**Au Caneton** ★★★
Big portions of famous local dishes make this half-timbered restaurant a must.
*32 rue Grande.*
*Tel: 02 31 32 73 32.*

### Pont-Audemer
**Auberge du Vieux Puits** ★★★
Classic beamed inn with quality food makes this a dream of Normandy come true.
*6 rue Notre-Dame-du-Pré.*
*Tel: 02 32 41 01 48.*

### Pont-l'Évêque
**Auberge de la Touques** ★★
Riverside restaurant with half-timbering. Serves Norman classics but only seats 20.
*Place Église.*
*Tel: 02 31 64 01 69.*

### Rouen
**Le Beffroy** ★★★
A gem in a backstreet, thanks to Odile Engel's down-to-earth cooking.
*15 rue Beffroy.*
*Tel: 02 35 71 55 27.*

**La Couronne** ★★★
Claims to be the oldest *auberge* in France, and has survived the tourist invasion.
*31 place Vieux-Marché.*
*Tel: 02 35 71 40 90.*

**Gill** ★★★★
Modern, exciting cooking by Gilles Tournadre makes him the top chef in town. For gourmands, this is a must.
*9 quai Bourse.*
*Tel: 02 35 71 16 14.*

### St-Aubin-sur-Mer
**Le Saint-Aubin** ★★
A perfect halt for seafood in the D-Day Beaches tour.
*Place du Canada.*
*Tel: 02 31 97 30 39.*

### St-Vaast-la-Hougue
**Les Fuschias** ★★
Imaginative preparation of seafood dishes in this hotel dining room.
*20 rue Maréchal-Foch.*
*Tel: 02 33 54 42 26.*

### Sées
**Le Dauphin** ★★★
Nice old restaurant in a nice old hotel. The very substantial helpings are well worth the price.
*31 place des Anciennes Halles.*
*Tel: 02 33 27 80 70.*

### Le Tréport
**Le Saint-Yves** ★★
Sensibly priced three-course menus in traditional style.
*Place Pierre Semart.*
*Tel: 02 35 86 34 66.*

### Trouville
**Les Vapeurs** ★★★
The jolly bistro where the Deauville stars like to slum it. Good fun.
*160 blvd Moureaux.*
*Tel: 02 31 88 15 24.*

### Vimoutiers
**La Couronne** ★★
A useful restaurant near Camembert, serving country dishes.
*9 rue du 8 Mai.*
*Tel: 02 33 39 03 04.*

### Vire
**Manoir de la Pommeraie** ★★
Local dishes served with a twist of imagination. Garden tables in summer.
*At Roullours, 2km south-east. Tel: 02 31 68 07 71.*

The many fields full of the distinctive spotted Normandy cattle prove that dairy products are an important part of Norman life. The soil and climate are ideal for milk production and the region is famous for its butter, cheese and cream.

The numerous small dairy farmers belong to large cooperatives, with modern processing and packaging plants which produce and market Normandy products not just throughout France but worldwide. The best-known cooperative, Isigny Sainte-Mère, today includes hundreds of farmers and came about from a merger between the Isigny-sur-Mer and Sainte-Mère-Eglise cooperatives.

Since 1986, Isigny's butter and *crème fraîche*, the thick, slightly acid soured cream from the region, have been protected by Appellation d'Origine Control (AOC) status. Nearly half of Isigny's production is now exported. Perhaps the most satisfying way to taste Normandy butter is straight from the churn at the local market. It is

Normandy's local cheeses that are responsible for the region's international fame as a dairy producer.

### Camembert

Normandy's most famous cheese is imitated worldwide, but authentic Camembert de Normandie AOC is made from unpasteurised milk. Two and a half litres (5 pints) of milk go into each 250-g (½-pound) flat disk, which is slightly salted before a month's maturation. Boxes labelled AOC contain 'real' camembert, which may have a characteristic red tint at the edges, surrounded by the usual soft white mould. Eaten soft, but not runny, and at room temperature, it is best accompanied by a glass of cider or a soft, fruity wine.

### Pont-l'Évêque

This is arguably Normandy's oldest cheese, dating at least to the 13th century. Three litres (6 pints) of milk make a 10-cm (4-inch) square block that is regularly washed in cold salted water. Matured for up to six weeks, its hearty aroma is delightfully redolent of sweet hay and hazelnut. Cut it diagonally but do not eat the golden/orange crust. Again, true Pont-l'Évêque bears the AOC label. Eat with a strong red wine.

## Livarot

Another medieval cheese, Livarot is nicknamed the 'colonel' thanks to the five stripes of reed tied round its middle. Five litres (10 pints) of milk go into this strong cheese that can be ripened for some three months. Trim its sticky orange rind, and savour its robust aromas and flavours – barn, onion and, yes, even milk. Accompany with a dry cider or robust red wine.

## Pavé d'Auge

Related to Pont-l'Évêque, the *pavé* (paving stone) is bigger, deeper and

needs 6 litres (13 pints) of milk before maturing for three months. The result smells earthy and tastes strong; only a full-bodied red wine can accompany it.

## Le Neufchâtel de Bray

Production of this cheese takes place only within a 30-km (19-mile) radius of Neufchâtel-en-Bray, north of the River Seine. A fresher, less fatty cheese than Camembert, it needs 1 litre (2 pints) of milk for 150g (5 ounces), matured for 10 days. Whether shaped in *coeurs* (hearts), *bondons* or *bondards* (like the *bonde* or bung of a cider barrel) or square *briquettes*, the taste is the same. Less mature cheeses have a crumbly, almost fluffy chalk-white centre that melts in the mouth – ask for it *pas trop fait*. Or, for a centre more akin to Camembert, ask for it *fait au coeur*.

Sampling fine cheese is an essential part of any visit to Normandy

# Hotels and accommodation

As a tourist destination since the early 19th century, Normandy's coast has hundreds of hotels. Some are grand and famous like the Normandy at Deauville, others are members of modern chains, dotted round the edges of the larger towns. Then there are the ancient inns that have been receiving guests for centuries, like the Lion d'Or in Bayeux, the burgeoning *chambres d'hôtes* (bed and breakfasts) and, of course, self-catering apartments.

Hotel with character, rue Martainville, Rouen

Unless you are travelling during July, August and early September, it is rarely difficult to find a room at the price and standard you require. During the summer holidays, however, advance reservations are essential as most of Paris seems to head for Normandy.

## Pricing

Lodgings are surprisingly inexpensive in France compared to similar hotels in the US or UK. For a no-frills budget traveller, ask the tourist office to point out family-run hotels without any stars, where rooms may go below €30 per night. Even elegant rooms in châteaux may only cost €200–300 for the full experience. Chain hotels, in town centres or by the roadside, are more moderate from €60–120 per night.

## Rating system

There are five grades of hotel in France, from the simplicity of 1-star to the top of the range 4-star *luxe*, luxury establishment. These stars reflect the range of facilities rather than quality, so

a comfortable, friendly 2-star hotel may be more to your liking than a more formal 4-star hotel which has porters, receptionists and a swimming pool. The French Government Tourist Office has branches all over the world, often known as La Maison de la France, where full listings of hotels in Normandy are available.

Their annual magazine, *The Traveller in France Reference Guide*, published in Britain, has hundreds of hotel listings along with reservation numbers. Among the most popular hotel chains are:

**Logis de France**
Some 4,000 family-run hotels in France, mainly in the 1- and 2-star category; listing published annually in March.
*Tel: (020) 7287 3181 (UK);*
*(1) 45 84 83 84 (France).*
*www.logis-de-france.fr/uk*
**Châteaux et Hôtels Indépendants**
The name spells it out: over 460 hotels with a special ambience.
*Tel: (1) 40 07 00 20 (France).*
*www.chateauxhotels.com*

### Relais & Châteaux
150 luxury hotels, often in old castles or country mansions. Book on sale.
*Tel: (1) 45 72 96 50 (France).*
*www.relaischateaux.com.*
*Tel: 00 800 2000 0002 (UK)*

### Balladins
80 1-star modern hotels all over France.
*Tel: (1) 60 38 11 84 (France).*
*www.balladins.com*

### Campanile
350 modern, motel-style hotels across France.
*Tel: (020) 8569 6969 (UK);*
*(1) 64 62 46 46 (France).*
*www.envergure.fr/campanile*

### Nuit d'Hôtel
Over 50 budget-price, modern hotels.
No star, but cheap and clean.
*Tel: (1) 64 46 05 05 (France).*

### Ibis-Arcade
400 modern hotels at 2-star level, all over France.
*Tel: (020) 8283 4500 (UK);*
*(1) 69 91 05 63 (France).*
*www.ibishotel.com*

### Resthotel Primevère
160 modern 2-star hotels, usually on the outskirts of large towns.
*Tel: (05) 90 85 36 (France, free call).*

Once in France, it is well worth stopping at an Office de Tourisme or Syndicat d'Initiative (tourist office) for further suggestions. Some will even help you with reservations.

### Chambres d'Hôtes
As in the rest of France, this sign has become a familiar sight in Normandy, where more and more private homes are offering bed and breakfast. Some serve just the traditional coffee and bread or croissant, others offer cheese and sausage for German and Dutch tastes. Signs proclaiming 'B&B' or 'English breakfast' indicate just how many British visitors cross the English Channel; the Normans recognise that even more are arriving via the Channel Tunnel. For advance booking, the network Bienvenue à la Ferme can help you find a nice place in the country.
*Tel: 01 53 57 11 44.*
*www.bienvenue-a-la-ferme.com*

### Self-catering
Thousands of French and foreign visitors prefer to rent a cottage and cater for themselves. These include country houses, often with real character and charm. The nationwide Gîtes de France organisation lists all the available properties in a thick yellow book. It is vital to book several months in advance since holiday periods get booked up, particularly for seaside locations.
*Tel: (0990) 360360 (UK); (1) 47 42 20 20 (France). www.gites-de-france.fr*

An establishment making itself known to non-French speakers

# On business

The French are quite conservative about doing business, especially outside the major cities. Allow plenty of time for appointments and don't try to rush through schemes. The Normans are considered more conservative than most. The best time for an appointment is mid-morning or mid-afternoon. Business lunches may be the way of the world in North America and Britain but less so in France, where meals are considered a social pleasure. Use social meetings to make friendships, to put the client/customer at ease. Avoid broaching business until the coffee stage of a meal.

A good start for the business person – the local chamber of commerce

### Banking

French banking is somewhat different from banking in other EU member nations, and has a reputation for being old-fashioned, slow and stuffy.

Outside the major cities, banks are not well versed in dealing internationally. Many overseas visitors prefer to use multinational banks that have infiltrated France as EU deregulation has grown.

### Business hotels

International chain hotels with good communications facilities include:

**Caen**
**Holiday Inn City:** *place Foch.*
*Tel: 02 31 27 57 57.*
**Mercure:** *1 place Courtonne.*
*Tel: 02 31 47 24 24.*
**Novotel:** *ave Côte de Nacre.*
*Tel: 02 31 43 42 00.*
**Cherbourg**
**Mercure:** *Gare Maritime.*
*Tel: 02 33 44 01 11.*

**Le Havre**
**Mercure:** *Chaussée d'Angoulême.*
*Tel: 02 35 19 50 50.*
**Rouen**
**Mercure:** *Rouen Centre, rue Croix de Fer.*
*Tel: 02 35 52 69 52.*
**Mercure:** *Rouen Champ de Mars, ave Aristide Briand.*
*Tel: 02 35 52 42 32.*
**Novotel:** *Rouen Sud Le Madrillet, St-Etienne-du-Rouvray.*
*Tel: 02 35 66 58 50.*

### Conferences

Conferences and incentive travel are well catered for in Normandy, with a range of facilities and specialist offices in each *département*.

**Upper Normandy**
**Chambre Régionale de Commerce et d'Industrie de Haute-Normandie**,
*9 rue Robert Schumann, BP124 76002 Rouen Cedex.*
*Tel: 02 35 88 44 42;*
*fax: 02 35 88 06 52.*

**Lower Normandy**
**Chambre Régionale de Commerce et d'Industrie de Basse-Normandie**,
*1 rue René Cassin, Saint-Contest, 14911 Caen Cedex 9. Tel: 02 31 54 40 40; fax: 02 31 54 40 41.*
**Pays de la Loire (covering Sarthe and Mayenne)**
*CDT Pays de la Loire, 2 rue de la Loire, 44200 Nantes. Tel: 02 40 48 24 20; fax: 02 40 08 07 10.*

### Conventions and seminars

Normandy has a growing reputation for congress and seminar facilities, not only at seaside resorts but also in historic cities where many of the older buildings can be hired for special functions. The local tourist offices have full details.

### Credit cards

Most French shops and restaurants accept major credit cards. The most popular is the Carte Bleue (part of Visa, Barclaycard and Bank Americard network).

### Internet

French internet use is in a period of exponential growth. While only larger business hotels may come wired, public pay or free terminals may be found at post offices, libraries, hotel lobbies and at internet and networked games cafés.

### Media

Rouen and Caen are the main publishing centres for press with an economic slant.
*La Lettre de la Haute-Normandie* is published every Wednesday, dealing with local economic and political issues (*tel: 02 35 89 78 00*).

*La Lettre du Développement Local en Normandie* is a monthly round-up of local business prospects. Subscription only (*tel: 02 35 89 78 00*).
*Normandie Magazine* rounds up what it calls Anglo-Norman news each month. Published in St-Lô in both English and French (*tel: 02 33 77 32 70. www.normandie-magazine.fr*).
*La Lettre de Basse-Normandie* is a weekly round-up of local and political issues that is published from Caen (*tel: 02 31 75 30 60*).

### Meeting and greeting

The formality of shaking hands is very important; the technique is one decisive shake downward. When a group of farmers meets at the market you will see everyone shake hands. The same applies in an office; it is advisable to shake every hand on arrival and departure. Always dress formally: the French judge a person by the way he or she dresses.

### Minitel

This is a computer keyboard and terminal that hooks into the telephone allowing owners access to thousands of facts and figures, from share prices to the telephone directory.

### Opening hours

The two-hour lunch hour is standard throughout France.
**Offices:** 8am–12.30pm; 2.30–5pm.
**Banks:** 9am–noon; 1.30–4.30pm.
(Banks close at noon on the eve of an official holiday.)
**Government offices:** 9am–noon; 2–6pm.
**Business premises:** Often closed on Mondays in rural areas.

# Practical guide

## Arriving

European Union residents visiting France need only a passport to enter the country. Citizens of the USA, Canada, New Zealand and most other western European nations need no visa for a stay of less than three months. Australians and South Africans need a visa irrespective of the length of their stay.

Travellers who require visas should obtain them in their country of residence, as it may prove difficult to obtain them elsewhere.

## By air

Normandy has five airports with inter-national connections: Caen, Cherbourg, Deauville, Le Havre and Rouen.

## By ferry

There are numerous regular ferries from Normandy to the UK: St Malo (for westernmost Normandy), Cherbourg, Caen, Ouistreham, Le Havre and Dieppe. The companies are Brittany Ferries, P&O Portsmouth and Condor Ferries.

Irish Ferries have sailings from Rosslare to Cherbourg.

## By road

The fast Autoroute de Normandie starts from Paris in the east, follows the Seine to the south, before turning west and running inland from the coast to Caen, where it has been extended towards Bayeux and on to Cherbourg. The route from Calais and Boulogne to Rouen and Caen is also motorway all the way. A new autoroute now runs between Rouen and Alençon, passing by Lisieux and

Sées. Tolls are payable, calculated on the basis of distance travelled.

## By train

Normandy is well served by train, with fast links to Paris, as well as from all the Channel ferry ports and the Channel Tunnel.

*The Thomas Cook European Timetable*, which is published monthly and gives up-to-date details of most European rail services and many shipping services through Europe, will help you plan a rail journey to, from and around France. It is available to buy online at *www.thomascookpublishing.com*, from some stations in the UK and from any branch of Thomas Cook (or by phoning *00 44 1733 416477*). In the USA, contact Rail Europe for schedule, route and pass information. *Tel: 1-877-257-2887. www.raileurope.com*

## Camping and caravanning

Normandy has many fine campsites, each graded by the tourist boards who rate the number of facilities on offer, from one- to four-star.

The French love the great outdoors and almost every village has a campsite. For detailed information about camping contact the local tourist offices or: Fédération Française de Camping et de Caravanning (*78 rue de Rivoli, 75004 Paris, tel: (1) 42 72 84 08*).

Caravans should maintain a distance of 50m (164ft) between vehicles, have proper rear-view mirrors and be within the maximum dimensions of 11m (36ft) in length and 2.5m (8ft) in width.

## Children

Children are a natural and welcome part of any holiday in France. Most can sleep in their parents' bedroom free or for a low supplement. They are welcome in restaurants where children's menus are prevalent, as are high chairs. Only the most up-market restaurants would turn a hair at the sight of a family invasion.

When travelling by train, ask for discounts: children under four travel free; from four to 12, at half-price.

## Climate

Normandy's lush green pastures are the result of rain. The damp climate is sometimes warmer than expected, as the Gulf Stream touches the Cotentin Peninsula near Cherbourg. However, with only about two hours of winter sun every day in Cherbourg, it is obvious that summer is the best time to visit.

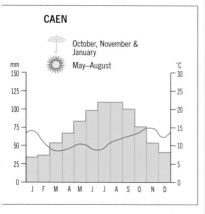

**CAEN**

October, November & January

May–August

mm
150

125

100

75

50

25

0

J F M A M J J A S O N D

°C
30

25

20

15

10

5

0

**Weather Conversion Chart**
25.4mm = 1 inch
°F = 1.8 x °C + 32

Spring is brisk, autumn mellow with chilly, fire-side evenings; the winter decidedly raw.

Caen, for example, averages 13°C (55°F) in April, jumps to 22°C (72°F) in July and August and slumps back to 15°C (59°F) in October. The rain comes mainly in the autumn. The best time for touring by car is April and May, when the apple blossom is at its best.

## Conversion tables

*See p183.* France has its own dress sizes, but shoes and all menswear follow the rest of Europe.

## Crime

Normandy is quiet and peaceful, but never offer the temptation of visible valuables in the car. At the height of the season, handbags are always at risk in crowds.

## Customs regulations

As Normandy is part of the European Union, visitors from its member countries benefit from new regulations introduced in 1993. The amount of duty-paid goods (those bought in local shops) you can take home from Normandy is only restricted by notional limits, above which you may be asked to prove that your purchases are for personal use rather than your own commercial use.

If you are aged 17 or over you can bring back: 800 cigarettes, 400 cigarillos, 200 cigars, 1kg of tobacco, 90 litres of wine, 10 litres of spirits, 20 litres of fortified wine and 100 litres of beer.

As of 1999, duty-free allowances were abolished within the EU and travellers whose journey begins and ends in an EU country are no longer eligible. Visitors to Normandy from non-EU countries are still eligible.

The allowances here are (per person aged over 17): 200 cigarettes or 100 cigarillos or 50 cigars or 250g of tobacco; 1 litre of spirits or 2 litres of table wine and 2 litres of fortified or sparkling wine; 75g of perfume.

These limits may vary from time to time so it is best to check when you make your purchase; current limits are posted in duty-free shops.

**Driving**

Driving licences from all European Union countries are valid in France, as are US, Canadian, Australian and New Zealand licences. Drivers should always carry the vehicle's registration documents and valid insurance papers. The so-called 'green card', the International Insurance Certificate, is also highly recommended, as is a home-based breakdown/accident scheme.

In France you drive on the right, and road signs are international. Although *priorité à droite* (priority for cars approaching from the right) still applies in built-up areas, the rule no longer applies on roundabouts. Dipped headlights should be used in poor visibility and, of course, at night. Right-hand drive vehicles should use patches on the headlights to prevent dazzle, though yellow tinting is no longer a requirement. If seat belts are fitted, their use is compulsory, as are helmets for motorcyclists.

Car rental is easy in Normandy, with all the major international companies

such as Avis, Budget, Europcar and Hertz represented in the bigger towns; Citer-Eurodollar is a reliable French company.

**Speed limits**

Urban areas: 50kph (31mph).
Single carriageway roads: 90kph (56mph) (on wet roads: 80kph/50mph).
Dual carriageway roads: 110kph (68mph) (on wet roads: 100kph/62mph).
Motorways: 130kph (81mph) (on wet roads: 110kph/68mph).
Note: a minimum speed of 80kph (50mph) applies when overtaking in the middle lane.
Motorcycles with less than 80cc have a 75kph (47mph) speed limit.

**Road signs**

*Rappel* is a reminder of speed limit restrictions.
Blue signs indicate motorways.
Green signs indicate main roads.
White signs indicate local roads.
Green signs with *Bis* in yellow are alternative quieter routes.
Yellow signs indicate a *déviation* (diversion).

**Electricity**

220 volts is the national standard, along with Continental-style plugs. Adaptors are worth buying before leaving home.

**Embassies**
**Australia**
*4 rue Jean Rey, 75015 Paris.*
*Tel: 01 40 59 33 00.*
**Canada**
*35 ave Montaigne, 75008 Paris.*
*Tel: 01 44 43 29 00.*

**Ireland**
*4 rue Rude, 75016 Paris.*
*Tel: 01 44 17 67 00.*
**New Zealand**
*7 ter rue Léonard de Vinci, 75016 Paris.*
*Tel: 01 45 01 43 43.*
**UK** (Consular Office)
*18 bis rue d'Anjou, 75008 Paris.*
*Tel: 01 44 51 31 02.*
**USA**
*2 ave Gabriel, 75008 Paris.*
*Tel: 01 43 12 22 22.*

## Emergency telephone numbers

**Accidents** Police Secours dial *17.*
**Directory Enquiries** *12.*
**European Emergency Number** *112* for direct access to French emergency services.
**Ambulance** SAMU dial *15*, or *02 35 88 44 22* – in Rouen.
**Chemist** ring police for *pharmaciens de garde* (duty chemist).
**Dentist** ring police for *dentiste de garde* (duty dentist).
**Breakdown** GB Assistance, Caen.
*Tel: 02 31 75 26 00.*
**Doctor** SOS Médecins:
Calvados *tel: 02 31 34 31 31.*
Rouen *tel: 02 35 03 03 30.*
**Fire** Sapeurs Pompiers *18.*
**Poison** Centre Anti-Poisons, Caen and Rouen. *Tel: 02 35 88 44 00.*

## Health and insurance

There are no mandatory vaccination requirements, and no vaccination recommendations other than to keep tetanus and polio immunisation up to date. Like every other part of the world, AIDS is present. Food and water are safe.

### Conversion Table

| FROM | TO | MULTIPLY BY |
|---|---|---|
| Inches | Centimetres | 2.54 |
| Feet | Metres | 0.3048 |
| Yards | Metres | 0.9144 |
| Miles | Kilometres | 1.6090 |
| Acres | Hectares | 0.4047 |
| Gallons | Litres | 4.5460 |
| Ounces | Grams | 28.35 |
| Pounds | Grams | 453.6 |
| Pounds | Kilograms | 0.4536 |
| Tons | Tonnes | 1.0160 |

To convert back, for example from centimetres to inches, divide by the number in the third column.

### Men's Suits

| | | | | | | | |
|---|---|---|---|---|---|---|---|
| UK | 36 | 38 | 40 | 42 | 44 | 46 | 48 |
| Rest of Europe | 46 | 48 | 50 | 52 | 54 | 56 | 58 |
| USA | 36 | 38 | 40 | 42 | 44 | 46 | 48 |

### Dress Sizes

| | | | | | | |
|---|---|---|---|---|---|---|
| UK | 8 | 10 | 12 | 14 | 16 | 18 |
| France | 36 | 38 | 40 | 42 | 44 | 46 |
| Italy | 38 | 40 | 42 | 44 | 46 | 48 |
| Rest of Europe | 34 | 36 | 38 | 40 | 42 | 44 |
| USA | 6 | 8 | 10 | 12 | 14 | 16 |

### Men's Shirts

| | | | | | | | |
|---|---|---|---|---|---|---|---|
| UK | 14 | 14.5 | 15 | 15.5 | 16 | 16.5 | 17 |
| Rest of Europe | 36 | 37 | 38 | 39/40 | 41 | 42 | 43 |
| USA | 14 | 14.5 | 15 | 15.5 | 16 | 16.5 | 17 |

### Men's Shoes

| | | | | | | |
|---|---|---|---|---|---|---|
| UK | 7 | 7.5 | 8.5 | 9.5 | 10.5 | 11 |
| Rest of Europe | 41 | 42 | 43 | 44 | 45 | 46 |
| USA | 8 | 8.5 | 9.5 | 10.5 | 11.5 | 12 |

### Women's Shoes

| | | | | | | |
|---|---|---|---|---|---|---|
| UK | 4.5 | 5 | 5.5 | 6 | 6.5 | 7 |
| Rest of Europe | 38 | 38 | 39 | 39 | 40 | 41 |
| USA | 6 | 6.5 | 7 | 7.5 | 8 | 8.5 |

All EU countries have reciprocal arrangements for reclaiming the costs of medical services.

UK residents should obtain the European Health Insurance Card, available online at *www.ehic.org.uk*, by phone on *0845 606 2030*, or from Post Offices in the UK. Claiming is often a laborious and long-drawn-out process and you are only covered for medical care, not for emergency repatriation, holiday cancellation and so on. You are strongly advised to take out a travel insurance policy to cover all eventualities.

You can purchase such insurance through most travel agents.

### Holidays
**1 January** New Year's Day
**March/April, variable** Easter Monday
**1 May** Labour Day/May Day
**8 May** VE, Victory in Europe Day
**Mid-May, variable** Ascension Day
**Late May, variable** Whit Monday
**14 July** Bastille Day
**15 August** Assumption Day
**1 November** All Saints' Day
**11 November** Remembrance Day
**25 December** Christmas Day

School holidays are staggered so that resorts are not inundated at one time.

### Lost property
Report anything lost to the local police. For lost or stolen credit cards ring the following numbers in Paris:
**American Express** *Tel: (1) 47 77 72 00.*
**Diner's Club** *Tel: (1) 47 62 75 00.*
**Eurocard** *Tel: (1) 45 67 84 84.*
**JCB International** *Tel: (1) 42 86 06 01.*
**VISA International** *Tel: (1) 42 77 11 90.*

## LANGUAGE

### BASIC WORDS AND PHRASES
| | |
|---|---|
| yes | oui |
| no | non |
| please | s'il vous plaît |
| thank you | merci |
| excuse me | pardon |
| I am sorry | pardon |
| good morning | bonjour |
| good evening | bonsoir |
| good night | bonne nuit |
| goodbye | au revoir |
| I have | j'ai |
| it is . . . | c'est |
| Do you speak English? | Parlez-vous anglais? |
| I do not understand | Je ne comprends pas |
| a little | un peu |
| much/many | beaucoup |
| enough | assez |
| too much/many | trop |

### NUMBERS AND QUANTITY
| | |
|---|---|
| one | un |
| two | deux |
| three | trois |
| four | quatre |
| five | cinq |
| six | six |
| seven | sept |
| eight | huit |
| nine | neuf |
| ten | dix |

## OTHER PHRASES

| | |
|---|---|
| when | quand |
| yesterday | hier |
| today | aujourd'hui |
| tomorrow | demain |
| at what time . . .? | à quelle heure . . .? |
| where is . . .? | où est . . .? |
| here | ici |
| there | là |
| near | près |
| before | avant |
| in front of | devant |
| behind | derrière |
| opposite | en face de |
| right | à droite |
| left | à gauche |
| straight on | tout droit |
| car park | un parking |
| petrol station | un poste à essence |
| parking | stationnement |
| prohibited | interdit |
| bridge | le pont |
| street | la rue |
| bus stop | l'arrêt du bus |
| railway station | la gare |
| platform | le quai |
| ticket | un billet |
| ten métro tickets | un carnet |
| single ticket | un aller simple |

## DAYS OF THE WEEK

| | |
|---|---|
| Monday | lundi |
| Tuesday | mardi |
| Wednesday | mercredi |
| Thursday | jeudi |
| Friday | vendredi |
| Saturday | samedi |
| Sunday | dimanche |

## MONTHS

| | |
|---|---|
| January | janvier |
| February | février |
| March | mars |
| April | avril |
| May | mai |
| June | juin |
| July | juillet |
| August | août |
| September | septembre |
| October | octobre |
| November | novembre |
| December | décembre |

Station signpost

## Media
### Newspapers
Regional newspapers are more influential than the national papers. In Normandy, *Ouest-France* is on sale everywhere.

English-language dailies like *The European*, the *International Herald Tribune* and *USA Today* appear in larger towns alongside popular British dailies.

### Radio
Twiddle round the dial to find your choice of non-stop classical music (Radio Classique), pop or ethnic music, all on FM.

France Inter on long wave (1829) is the equivalent of BBC Radio 4, which can also be heard quite clearly in Normandy.

### Television
France has four state-owned channels and two private channels, but many hotels now have satellite channels piping in English, German and American news, sport and films.

## Money matters
In 2002, the euro replaced the French franc as the national currency. Hotels, larger restaurants and some shops in main tourist areas accept traveller's cheques in lieu of cash. Be sure to ask before making the purchase.

## Museums
National museums offer a 50 per cent reduction on Sundays, are closed on Tuesdays and are free to students under 18. Half-price entry is charged for 18- to 25-year-olds and the over-60s.

Municipal museums are free on Sundays, for those under 7 and over 60, and usually close on Mondays. *See also* Standard Opening Hours *below*.

## Opening hours
**Banks** 9am–noon; 2–4pm weekdays. Closed on either Saturday or Monday. Also banks close early before a major holiday.
**Post offices** 8am–7pm weekdays; 8am–noon Saturdays.
**Food shops** 7am–6.30 or 7.30pm. Some open on Sunday mornings.
**Other shops** 9 or 10am–6.30 or 7.30pm. Many will close half or all day on Monday, and close from noon–2pm in small towns and villages.
**Hypermarkets** These popular centres usually stay open until 9pm or later from Monday to Saturday.

### Standard opening hours
There is a bewildering variety of opening hours but, in general, everywhere is open daily during July and August. The problem is that some famous buildings are maintained by the state, others by the region, a few by the town and a handful privately. Each has different ideas about when to open.

The major châteaux, churches and museums tend to open from 10am to 6pm, with two hours for lunch; most close for all or part of Monday or Tuesday.

Ruined castles and abbeys are open during daylight hours, often until 7pm in summer but closing at 4pm in winter. Surprisingly, many are closed on national holidays. Basically, the more commercial the attraction, the more it is open. Do phone ahead when planning a specific outing, particularly if you want a guided tour. (*See opposite*, Museums.)

## Pharmacies
Pharmacies are often identified by a green cross outside the shop. Contact the police (*see* Emergency Telephone Numbers, *p183*) for the duty pharmacist after hours.

## Places of worship
Normandy is predominantly Catholic, though there are some Protestant churches. There are synagogues in the larger towns and cities. Hotels and tourist offices have details of services.

## Post Offices
*Bureaux de poste* (post offices) are open Monday to Friday 8am–7pm and Saturday 8am–noon. Stamps can also be bought in a *tabac* (tobacconist). Post boxes are yellow, free-standing or set into a wall.

## Public transport
SNCF (French Railways) have reasonable fares and clean trains. Fares depend on colour-coded time periods: red, white and blue (the cheapest). Tickets must be validated (*composté*) with a time clock before departure.

Autocars are buses run by SNCF (train fares apply). Regular buses are limited to cities.

## Senior citizens
Produce a passport to take advantage of any discounts, irrespective of whether or not you are a French national.

## Student accommodation
Auberges de Jeunesse (Youth Hostels) abound in France. Their French headquarters are at 27 rue Pajol, 75018 Paris (*tel: (1) 44 89 87 27*).

International handbooks list French hostels for members.

## Sustainable tourism
Thomas Cook is a strong advocate of ethical and fairly traded tourism and believes that the travel experience should be as good for the places visited as it is for the people who visit them. That's why we firmly support The Travel Foundation, a charity that develops solutions to help improve and protect holiday destinations, their environment, traditions and culture. To find out what you can do to make a positive difference to the places you travel to and the people who live there, please visit:
*www.thetravelfoundation.org.uk*

## Telephones
Although coin-operated phone booths still exist, the *télécarte* (phone card) is taking over rapidly. Buy one in a post office or *tabac* to save time, trouble and money. The cards (50 units and 120 units) are much cheaper than a hotel call and simple to use.

Cheap rates operate between 10.30pm and 8am, after 2pm on Saturday and all day Sunday.

For an international call, dial *00*, then the country code:
**Australia** *61*; **Canada:** *1*; **Ireland** *353*; **New Zealand** *64*; **UK** *44*; **USA** *1*.

## Time

Normandy is on GMT plus 1 hour in winter, GMT plus 2 hours in summer. When it is noon in winter in Normandy, it is:

9pm in Canberra, Australia;
11am in Dublin, Ireland;
11am in London, England;
6am in Ottawa, Canada;
6am in Washington DC, USA;
11pm in Wellington, New Zealand.

## Tipping

Cafés and restaurants include all taxes and tips on their bills, although it is common to leave your coin change as a token. However, after an extended stay at a hotel, it is customary to leave a tip for the chambermaid. Porters, museum guides, taxi drivers and cinema usherettes welcome a *pourboire* (tip).

## Toilets

There are public toilets in department stores, cafés and restaurants, as well as the concrete self-cleaning *toilettes* (coin-operated booths) on the streets.

## Tourist offices

For general information on Normandy contact: **Comité Régional de Tourisme**, *Le Doyenné, 14 rue Charles Corbeau, 27000 Évreux. Tel: 02 32 33 79 00. www.normandy-tourism.org*

Each *département* has its own head office:
**Calvados** *CDT, place du Canada, 14000 Caen. Tel: 02 31 27 90 30. www.calvados-tourisme.com*
**Eure** *CDT de L'Eure, 3 rue du Commandant Letellier, 27003 Évreux. Tel: 02 32 62 04 27.*

**Manche** *CDT, Maison du Département, 50008 St-Lô CEDEX. Tel: 02 33 05 98 70.*
**Orne** *CDT, 88 rue Saint-Blaise, BP 50, 61002 Alençon CEDEX. Tel: 02 33 28 88 71.*
**Seine-Maritime** *CDT, 6 rue Couronné, BP60, 76420 Bihorel-lès-Rouen. Tel: 02 35 12 10 10.*
**Sarthe** *CDT, 19 bis rue del'Etoile, 72000 Le Mans. Tel: 02 43 40 22 50.*
**Mayenne** *CDT, BP 343, 84 avenue Robert-Buron, 53014 Laval CEDEX. Tel: 02 43 53 18 18.*

## Trains touristiques

You are never too old to enjoy a ride on a train, particularly if it is pulled by a steam engine and chugs through pretty countryside. Check with local tourist offices for timetables.

Several lines operate occasionally but many have recently stopped running. A line from Pacy-sur-Ewe to Breuilpont and Cocherel runs on Sundays and some other days in summer, using historic trains (*open: all year round, tel: 33 2 32 36 04 63).*

## Travellers with disabilities

Access to the major tourist attractions is improving all the time. However, as most of Normandy's attractions are ancient castles and cathedrals, there are often real problems for wheelchair visitors. Although there are no overall guides for the region, the **Comité National Français de Liaison pour la Réadaption des Handicapés** (CNFLRH), *236 bis, rue de Tolbiac, 75013 Paris (tel: (1) 53 80 66 66)* has leaflets (in French) on aspects of daily life in France.

**ACKNOWLEDGEMENTS**

Thomas Cook Publishing wishes to thank the following photographers, libraries and associations for their assistance in the preparation of this book.

JOHN MILES 120b
ERIC PARKS 16, 45, 75, 80a, 94, 110a, 153
JULIETTE ROGERS 13, 15, 17, 111a, 124
STILLMAN ROGERS 89, 90a
SPENCER ZAWASKY 92b, 95, 110b
NEIL SETCHFIELD 40
PICTURES COLOUR LIBRARY 22a, 28, 35, 44, 55, 61, 63, 67, 90b, 101, 105, 106b, 107, 108, 112a, 127, 136, 170, 172
SPECTRUM COLOUR LIBRARY 135a

The remaining pictures are held in the AA PHOTO LIBRARY and were taken by: ROB MOORE, with the exception of pages 134, 150, 151, 165, 166 which were taken by STEVE DAY; pages 146a, 148b which were taken by ANTONY SOUTER; and page 174b taken by BARRIE SMITH.

**Index**: MARIE LORIMER

**Proofreading**: JAN McCANN for CAMBRIDGE PUBLISHING MANAGEMENT LIMITED

Send your thoughts to
# books@thomascook.com

We're committed to providing the very best up-to-date information in our travel guides and constantly strive to make them as useful as they can be. You can help us to improve future editions by letting us have your feedback. If you've made a wonderful discovery on your travels that we don't already feature, if you'd like to inform us about recent changes to anything that we do include, or if you simply want to let us know your thoughts about this guidebook and how we can make it even better – we'd love to hear from you.

Send us ideas, discoveries and recommendations today and then look out for your valuable input in the next edition of this title. And, as an extra 'thank you' from Thomas Cook Publishing, you'll be automatically entered into our exciting monthly prize draw.

Emails to the above address, or letters to Travellers Project Editor, Thomas Cook Publishing, PO Box 227, Unit 18, Coningsby Road, Peterborough PE3 8SB, UK.

Please don't forget to let us know which title your feedback refers to!